Praise from Scouters and Parents for
The Eagle Court of Honor Book

I bought your book and honored my son's wishes to not carbon-copy the previous ceremonies as our troop usually does. We got so many compliments, even from long-time Scouters in the program, about how special the ceremony had been. It was one of the happiest and proudest days of my life.

Babette Arroyo

The Eagle Court of Honor Book is an excellent resource for any troop and any Scout leader. This book succinctly provides a wealth of information about how to put on an Eagle court of honor. It includes planning ideas, complete program scripts, and lots of inspiration. The book is the perfect resource to hand to parents who want ideas, structure, and words to say without becoming overwhelmed. Written in a clear, concise, and very readable style, *The Eagle Court of Honor* book is an essential addition to your troop library. You can spend hours on the internet getting ideas or 30 minutes learning everything you need to know from this book.

Rob Faris

The information is insightful and a welcome addition for our parents preparing for their sons' ceremony. It is well organized and easy to follow. It flows like a river.

Caren Barone

As a frequent visitor to Eagle Scout courts of honor, I can honestly say that more folks ought take the opportunity to review Mark Ray's masterpiece. Our Scouts deserve the best, they deserve a unique experience, and they deserve to be surrounded by folks who have enjoyed simple and stress-free planning for the event. I'll take 10 copies!

Corey Kline

The planning documents and explanation for each part of the different ceremonies are very useful and are well thought out. This is definitely a nice addition to my library of references for Scouting.

David Blackburn

This book is a great resource for those who are new to planning Eagle courts of honor or for those who want to add something a little different than the rote items they normally do. When the Scoutmaster of a neighboring troop needed help with her son's Eagle ceremony, I gladly gave her my copy, knowing it was a wonderful resource. I then purchased another copy for myself! I believe that speaks for the quality and usefulness of this book.

Ida H. Lively

Your book … is terrific. I know stuff is available online, but this was in our hands and just so helpful.

Terri Stevens

[My son] Thomas had grown bored with the "traditional" ceremony used in the troop, so he used your book to design his own. He read the book cover to cover and then set out on planning his ceremony. You would not believe how many parents, Scouts, and adults have commented about his being the "best" ceremony they have ever attended.

Leta D. Walton

There are so many Eagle materials available online that it can be overwhelming to try and sift through the options and information. Thank heavens I invested in this gem of a book! As the mother of two Eagle Scouts, *The Eagle Court of Honor Book* was my survival guide for the planning of their ceremonies. Time management, suggested scripts, basic information you need to know, and so much more!

Kathy Caudill

THE EAGLE COURT OF HONOR BOOK

★ *The* ★

EAGLE
COURT
of HONOR
BOOK

★ THIRD EDITION ★

Mark Ray

Illustrated by Lloyd R. Lotz, Sr.

Also by the Author

The Scoutmaster's Other Handbook

Growing Up Right, Growing Up Strong: Parents, Kids, and Scouting
(coauthored with Dan Baker, Ph.D.)

Ready to Go Devotions for Mission and Service

Cover photo copyright © 2011 by Ken Canning.

Third edition, third printing: March 2013

The Eagle Court of Honor Book is not an official publication of the Boy Scouts of America.

ISBN: 978-0-9651207-4-6

Boy Scouts of America Catalog Number: 614446

For three of the Eagle Scouts in my life:
T.J. Ray, Ted Hitch, and Denny Gookin

and for my mother, who still wears her
Eagle Scout mother's pin

Contents

Preface to the Third Edition

In 1996, thinking I knew how to run Eagle Scout® court of honors, I published the first edition of this book. It featured three complete ceremonies, fourteen ceremony parts, and a design that's best forgotten.

To paraphrase Harry S Truman, I've learned a lot since I knew it all. As I've planned all sorts of ceremonies and heard from hundreds of Scouters and parents from around the country, I've refined and expanded the book, making "the complete guide to Scouting's greatest moment" more complete than ever.

One thing hasn't changed, however. As always, the purpose of this book is to help you plan the best possible Eagle court of honor for your new Eagle Scout. After all, you only get one chance.

You can use this book in many ways. If you're in the midst of planning a court of honor now, turn to Chapter 2, which describes the planning process in detail, and Chapter 7, which includes eight complete ceremony scripts. If you have a little more time, start with Chapter 1, which explains the purposes of the Eagle court of honor. If you need help with support functions like physical arrangements, decorations, and publicity, read Chapter 8.

A final note: If you have compliments, complaints, or contributions to make, please let me know. In 1996, I couldn't imagined publishing a third edition of *The Eagle Court of Honor Book*. Today, I can't imagine *not* publishing a fourth.

Mark Ray

Chapter 1

Introduction

The philosophy and purposes of
the Eagle court of honor

Introduction

A fond mother watches her boy where he stands,
Apart from his comrades tonight
As they place on his camp-battered tunic a badge,
An Eagle, the emblem of Right.
—*S. Kurtz Hingley*

Ask an adult Eagle Scout what he remembers most about Scouting®, and he'll likely tell you about campouts in the rain, perhaps a trip to Philmont or a national jamboree, and his Eagle Scout court of honor. He would probably agree with Eagle Scout and U.S. President Gerald Ford, who said, "One of the proudest moments of my life came in the court of honor when I was awarded the Eagle Scout badge."

That moment is what Norman Rockwell captured in his painting "A Great Moment." That moment is what S. Kurtz Hingley described in his wonderfully sentimental poem, quoted above.

That moment is what the boy will remember long after he becomes a man.

The Purposes of the Eagle Court of Honor

Unfortunately, from a logistical standpoint, that moment, the presentation of the Eagle badge, takes only ten or fifteen minutes and isn't all that impressive in and of itself. So Scouters have figured out ways over the years to stretch the badge presentation into a complete and quite impressive program, one that lasts an hour or so and puts the badge presentation into context for the people in the audience.

Whatever its length, of course, the primary purpose of the Eagle court of honor is to honor the new Eagle Scout. He should be the center of attention, and the spotlight should never stray far from him.

But the ceremony should fulfill other purposes as well. Besides presenting the Scout with a badge, it should also present him with a challenge: to use his skills and experience to be a leader in his troop and in his community. This challenge, or charge, helps him answer the question "Now what?" much as a commencement speech does for high-school graduates.

While the new Eagle is the focus of attention, a few other people, specifically his parents and Boy Scout™ leaders, should briefly share the spotlight. The honoree may be the one who climbed the trail to Eagle, but his Scout leaders and parents pushed him at least part of the way. By Scout leaders, incidentally, I mean not just the boy's Scoutmaster® and assistant Scoutmasters, but also his merit-badge counselors, Cubmaster, and den leaders.

Another purpose of the court of honor is to set an example for the other Scouts in the troop, as well as for any Cub Scouts or Webelos Scouts present. After an effective court of honor, every Scout will go home and check his handbook to see what he needs to do to earn his next rank.

Finally, the ceremony should inform and inspire all the family members, friends, Scout parents, chartered organization members, and other people in the audience. It's a wonderful time to tell the story of Scouting and get people charged up (or recharged). The ceremony has to touch and involve the people who attend. Otherwise, they'll feel like guests at a stranger's wedding – and they won't come back for the next court of honor.

A Tale of Two Audiences

The average court of honor has two audiences, not one. The first audience consists of the honoree's immediate family, fellow Scouts, and Scout leaders, all of whom are very familiar with what this Eagle Scout thing is all about.

The other audience consists of the honoree's aunts, uncles, cousins, friends, teachers, coaches, and neighbors – people who may not have a clue what it means to be an Eagle Scout.

As you're planning your court of honor, keep this second audience in mind. Be sure that the ceremony helps them understand the significance of your honoree's accomplishment. A great way to do that is by including a "Scouting segment" and an "Eagle segment" in the ceremony, as I'll discuss in Chapter 3.

A Special Ceremony for a Special Scout

If you've been reading carefully so far, you've no doubt caught the references to "the honoree," "the new Eagle Scout," and "his parents." Notice I haven't talked about "the other honorees" or "the Scouts who are receiving other rank badges at the same court of honor."

In my opinion, the Eagle Scout Award should generally be presented at a special court of honor held to honor a single new Eagle – not at a regular troop court of honor or multi-Eagle affair. Becoming an Eagle Scout is important enough that it deserves a special court of honor. What's more, as I'll discuss in a moment, the ceremony should be tailored to the individual recipient, which is difficult to do when several boys are being honored.

Having said that, however, I should point out that multi-Eagle courts of honor are sometimes appropriate. In fact, one of the best (and best-attended) courts of honor I ever ran featured six honorees. It worked well in large part because all six were seniors in high school, members of the same church, and close friends. If three of the honorees had been 13 years old and three had been 18, we wouldn't have held a joint ceremony. If most of them had just squeaked by while one or two had earned 60 or 70 merit badges, we would have explored other options. But for this particular group of Scouts, a joint ceremony worked – and worked well.

Attendance is another issue you have to consider. If you hold several ceremonies over the course of a few months, the law of diminishing returns says the later ceremonies will be less well attended. On the flip side, ceremonies that feature multiple honorees tend to draw a bigger

---

Opting for a Joint Court of Honor

Consider holding a joint ceremony if you can answer "yes" to all or most of these questions:

- Are the honorees brothers, cousins, or close friends?
- Are the honorees about the same age?
- Have the honorees had similar levels of involvement in Scouting?
- Would holding separate ceremonies hurt attendance (or would holding a joint ceremony boost attendance)?
- Have all the honorees and their parents agreed to have a joint ceremony?

audience, which can be important if the honorees are older and haven't been visible in the troop recently.

So the general rule is "One Eagle, one court of honor," but it's a rule that's made to be broken. The sidebar on page 4 should help you decide.

Fitting the Ceremony to the Scout

If you're going to devote a whole ceremony to a single Scout, and if you're really going to focus on that Scout and his accomplishments, it doesn't make sense to use an off-the-rack ceremony or the same script that you've used for the last three (or thirty) courts of honor. Yet that's what many troops do.

A truly effective court of honor is tailor-made for its honoree. And that means more than just putting "Congratulations, Steve!" on the cake. It means truly fitting the ceremony to the honoree.

If the new Eagle has been very active in the Order of the Arrow®, for example, plan an OA-themed ceremony. If his faith is important to him, hold the ceremony at his place of worship. If his father, uncle, and grandfather are all Eagles, get them involved in the ceremony.

This book contains several complete scripts for courts of honor, as do various websites and the BSA publication *Troop Program Resources*. They

---

A Quantity Quandary

So what should you do if you have a backlog of Eagle Scouts and need to hold several courts of honor in a short period of time? Try these ideas:

- Group the honorees where possible to reduce the number of ceremonies.
- Hold significantly different ceremonies at different times and locations to attract different crowds and sustain people's interest.
- Don't repeat any ceremony elements (other than the obvious things like the actual badge presentation).
- Encourage one or two Scouts to delay their ceremonies – perhaps those who are planning to have a lot of out-of-town guests who would need more time to make travel arrangements.
- Emphasize, with all the recipients, the importance of inviting school, church, and family friends to the court of honor.
- Be sure you're not responsible for leading multiple courts of honor!

are all good, but don't use them strictly as written. Instead, personalize them to make them fit the Scout you're honoring. Tell about the merit badges™ *he* earned, the leadership positions *he* held, *his* camp staff experience, and *his* Eagle Scout leadership service project.

If you're feeling really creative, ignore the sample scripts and write your own. Just keep in mind the old Outback Steakhouse slogan: "No rules. Just right."

Involving the Family

To fit the ceremony to the Scout requires a lot more time and effort than just using a canned script. It also requires more involvement from the Scout and his family, who should be consulted early and often during the planning process.

In my opinion, many troops take the idea of family involvement to the extreme by delegating the entire planning process to the parents. The Eagle court of honor is a troop function, which means the Scoutmaster, an assistant Scoutmaster, or a troop committee member should be in charge.

That said, family-planned ceremonies can work, provided the family gets plenty of support from troop leaders. One key to a successful family-planned ceremony is to make sure someone other than a family member manages the actual event. Dad shouldn't have to get up in the middle of

---

A Court of Honor Toolkit

If your troop delegates court-of-honor planning to the family, consider creating a toolkit with the following items:

- Sample invitations, programs, and scripts
- Sample letters to dignitaries, along with names and addresses
- A sample press release and your local newspaper's contact information
- A list of helpful websites
- A copy of *The Eagle Court of Honor Book* (of course!)
- Any other helpful materials you've discovered

Put everything in a three-ring binder – stick bulky materials in pocketed dividers – and loan it to each new Eagle Scout's family.

the ceremony to adjust the thermostat. Mom shouldn't spend her evening worrying about last-minute details like running to the kitchen to grab the ice cream.

Whether families in your troop play a big role or a little one, it's important that everyone understands exactly who's doing what. For example, the troop could be in charge of writing the script, recruiting presenters, and preparing the printed program, leaving the family in charge of invitations and the reception. (Chapter 2 includes a backdater where you can record these assignments.)

A Word about Varsity Scouting and Venturing

While the Eagle Scout Award is the highest rank in the Boy Scout program, some Scouts actually earn it in Varsity Scout® teams instead of Boy Scout troops. Still others become Eagle Scouts in Venturing® crews, which is permissible if they reached the First Class rank in Boy Scouting.

However, the vast majority of Scouts receive the award in Boy Scout troops, so this book primarily uses Boy Scout terms: Scoutmaster, senior patrol leader, troop, etc. That said, it would be easy enough to adapt any of the material in this book to a team or crew court of honor, often by simply substituting one term for another.

I've made suggestions along the way for adapting specific parts of the ceremony. If you have other suggestions for team and crew courts of honor, I'd love to hear from you.

Chapter 2

Planning the Court of Honor

A step-by-step guide to planning the perfect court of honor

Planning the Court of Honor

A slip-shod and carelessly run court of honor is distinctly dangerous to Scouting.
—The How Book of Scouting, *1938*

An old joke asks, "How do you eat an elephant?" The answer – "One bite at a time" – applies equally well to planning an Eagle court of honor. It's a big job, but you can do it. You just have to take it one step at a time.

On pages 12-13, you'll find a court of honor backdater, which is simply a step-by-step list of what you need to do and when you need to do it. I recommend that you photocopy these pages (or, even better, access the backdater online at **www.eaglebook.com**) and record both the target date and the person responsible for each item on the list.

The great thing about backdaters is that they put everything in chronological order; the bad thing is that they make it hard to see the relationship between different items on the list. So in this chapter, I'll talk you through the planning process.

First Things First

The first thing that must happen, of course, is that the Scout must pass his board of review. On that date, he is officially an Eagle Scout, although his application must still be reviewed by the local council and the national office of the Boy Scouts of America®.

You should talk to the person in your local council service center who handles Eagle applications to find out about local procedures; this could be the registrar, the office manager, or another support-staff member. Check back with him or her to find out when the application was submitted to the national office, and make sure you're notified when the application is approved or if unforeseen problems arise. (If notifications typically go to the Scoutmaster and you're the mom, you won't necessarily hear right away when the application is approved.)

Preliminary Planning

Now you're ready to start planning. As quickly as possible, schedule a meeting that includes you, the honoree and his parents, and the Scoutmaster. At this meeting, you need to decide where and when to hold the court of honor.

Setting a Date

Although the honoree's Eagle Scout credentials will probably come back from the national office within a few weeks – much faster than a decade ago – I think you should allow a little more time to allow for adequate planning and promotion. Choosing a date six to eight weeks out seems to work well.

What day of the week should you choose? Many troops hold Eagle courts of honor on their regular meeting night (in place of the normal troop meeting), which helps minimize conflicts and maximize attendance by troop members. On the other hand, you may want to consider a weekend afternoon if you expect out-of-town guests to attend. A third option is to piggyback on a troop event; you could hold the court of honor on Saturday afternoon after a service project or even during a campout or summer camp, assuming the site is accessible to guests from outside the troop. Whatever date you choose, be sure to avoid conflicts with major school, community, or chartered organization events and be sure to run your tentative date by the troop committee and patrol leaders council for approval.

Picking a Location

While the logical location may be your chartered organization or the facility where your troop holds regular courts of honor, don't limit your options. If you're planning a spring court of honor, your Scout camp's chapel or a local park's amphitheater might be the perfect location. (Just

Eagle Court of Honor Backdater

Photocopy this backdater and use it as a worksheet as you plan the court of honor. (You can find an interactive version at **www.eaglebook.com/free_backdater.htm**.) Give copies to all participants so they know what is expected of them.

Weeks	Date	Action	Assigned To
-8	_____	Board of review is held.	_____
-7	_____	Chairperson is selected.	_____
-7	_____	Chairperson meets with family to begin planning.	_____
-7	_____	Set date and time for court of honor.	_____
-7	_____	Secure location.	_____
-7	_____	Send or email confirmation letter to person in charge of location.	_____
-7	_____	Order invitations.	_____
-6	_____	Develop invitation list.	_____
-6	_____	Begin promoting the event within the troop.	_____
-5	_____	Order needed supplies from council (awards, program covers, etc.).	_____
-5	_____	Order plaques and other recognition items.	_____
-5	_____	Solicit congratulatory letters from public officials and other VIPs.	_____
-5	_____	Flesh out program and prepare script.	_____
-5	_____	Order NESA membership.	_____
-4	_____	Mail invitations.	_____
-4	_____	Recruit master of ceremonies and presenters.	_____
-4	_____	Recruit volunteers to coordinate support functions.	_____
-4	_____	Distribute scripts to presenters.	_____
-3	_____	Order refreshments.	_____

Days	Date	Action	Assigned To
-3	_____	Visit the court-of-honor location to check facilities.	_____
-2	_____	Have programs printed.	_____
-2	_____	Send press releases. If possible, include a photo.	_____
-2	_____	Call troop families to promote.	_____
-1	_____	Gather all necessary materials, props, awards, etc.	_____

Days	Date	Action	Assigned To
-2	_____	Hold a rehearsal with all presenters.	_____
-2	_____	Confirm attendance of all presenters.	_____
-1	_____	Confirm access to building.	_____
0	_____	Set up and decorate room.	_____
0	_____	Set heater or air conditioner.	_____
0	_____	Check all audio-visual equipment (microphones, projectors, etc.).	_____
0	_____	Make sure all awards and other props are in place.	_____
0	_____	Reserve seats for presenters, the honoree, and his family.	_____
0	_____	Set up refreshments.	_____
0	_____	Position greeters at the door(s) to hand out programs.	_____
0	_____	Check with presenters one last time.	_____
0	_____	THE COURT OF HONOR	_____
+1	_____	Send thank-you notes.	_____
+3	_____	Send write-up (with pictures) to newspapers.	_____
+5	_____	Evaluate the event and make notes for next time.	_____

be sure to have a rain plan.) If the honoree forged strong ties with the agency where he did his Eagle service project, consider holding the court of honor there. If you'd prefer a more formal setting (or you like "The Challenge" script in Chapter 7), see if you can use a courtroom at city hall. If you're honoring an Eagle Scout who's home from college and expect a small crowd, there's nothing wrong with holding the ceremony in someone's home. Find the right location for *your* ceremony.

Part of finding the right location is making sure it's the right size. An auditorium or sanctuary seems full when 85 percent of the seats are filled. Go higher than that, and people won't be able to find a seat. Go a lot lower than that, and the space will feel half empty. If you choose a room that's maybe 20 percent bigger than the crowd you expect, the space will feel comfortably full.

Once you've found the perfect location, make a reservation, pay any required deposit, and send or email a note to the person in charge of the facility to confirm the details. With the date and location confirmed, you can start recruiting presenters and promoting the court of honor.

Making Other Initial Decisions

At your initial meeting, find out what type of ceremony the family prefers. Ask them what ceremony elements they've seen at other courts of honor that they'd like to include (or want to avoid).

Learning by Example

"There is no teaching to compare with example." Those words from Lord Robert Baden-Powell, the founder of Scouting, came back to me at a court of honor conducted by another troop in our council. Being in the audience, instead of on stage, gave me the chance to watch and listen – and to learn things that will make my troop's courts of honor better in the future.

On the back of my program, I jotted down half a dozen ideas that the ceremony suggested. Some were things I'll try in the future, while others were things I definitely *won't* try because they just didn't work.

I encourage you to follow my example of following other people's example. Before you plan your next court of honor, attend a court of honor held by another troop. Make notes of what you like and what you don't, and incorporate that experience in your own ceremony.

Next, find out whether there are any particular people they want to include in the ceremony. For example, the honoree might want a former troop member who's now in college to serve as master of ceremonies, his Eagle Scout grandfather to give the Eagle charge, and his cousin who's a Tiger Cub to play some role. As you develop the script, you can start matching people with jobs. Be sure you know about any special family dynamics you need to consider (an out-of-town birth father who should be included alongside the mother and stepfather, for example).

Finally, decide who should recruit these people and what level of involvement the family will have in further planning. Discuss which expenses are the responsibility of the family, the troop, or the chartered organization.

The Invitation List

Early on, the family should start developing an invitation list. This list should include troop members, non-Scouting friends, other family members, godparents, religious leaders, teachers, coaches and band directors, Eagle board of review members, district and council VIPs, past Scout leaders, those who helped with the Eagle service project, and anyone else

---

Invitation List

People won't come to a court of honor if you don't invite them. Even members of the troop need an invitation. Here's a list to get you started.

Troop members and leaders	District executive
Representatives from the	District chairman
chartered organization	District commissioner
Past Scout leaders	Family members
Den leaders	Friends
Cubmasters	Neighbors
Merit-badge counselors	Godparents
Those who helped with the Eagle	Religious leaders
service project	Favorite teachers and coaches
Eagle board of review members	Members of the troop's sister Cub
Buddies from camp staff	Scout pack

who's played a part in the Scout's development. I've include a list in the box on the previous page to give you a head start.

Developing a good invitation list is especially important if the Eagle Scout is older or has not been highly visible within the troop recently. Take the case of a Scout who passes his board of review just before his eighteenth birthday and comes home from college for his court of honor. Many troop members won't know him well, so you'll have to work extra hard to boost attendance.

The parents will probably be responsible for ordering invitations, having them printed, and mailing them. Invitation cards are available from your local Scout Shop®, but you can also design your own if you wish.

Whoever creates them and however they're created, invitations should answer the five "W" questions: who, what, when, where, and why. "Who," of course, refers to the honoree, and "what" refers to the court of honor. "When" means the time and the date (including the day of the week), and "where" means the location. (If necessary, include a map; at the very least, include the street address. Not everybody knows where the First United Methodist Church is.) The final question, "why," is often overlooked. Somewhere in the invitation, indicate why the court of honor is such a significant event. Explain, for example, that only five percent of all Scouts become Eagles or that this will be the first Eagle court of honor in your troop's history. That little bit of explanation might convince people to attend your ceremony instead of vegging out on the couch.

Invitations and the Multi-Scout Court of Honor

How do you handle invitations for a multi-Scout court of honor? I recommend having the invitations printed jointly with all names listed and then letting each family send them out to their own list. While you might save a few stamps by consolidating invitation lists, it's much simpler to let each family doing their own mailing. A logical exception would be troop members; families could divide up the troop roster or troop members could be invited via the troop newsletter.

One advantage is that each Scout can include a personal note in the invitations he sends. (For example, one recipient might want to ask that any gifts to go to the agency his service project benefited.) Another advantage is that guests won't show up with a card or gift for the Scout who invited them but not for the other honorees, a small but annoying inconvenience.

I recommend including a photo of the honoree in uniform in the invitation. (It's also fun if you can include a photo of him as a Cub Scout!) Besides spiffing up the invitation, such a photo makes a great keepsake for the honoree and his family. You can also use it in a slideshow during the ceremony.

Sometimes the Eagle Scout adds a personal note when inviting relatives and other people who have been especially important to him. For out-of-town relatives, you might suggest a message like this one: "I know that it may not be practical for you to attend my court of honor. The purpose of sending this invitation is to let you know of my accomplishment. Achieving the Eagle Scout Award is very special to me, and I wanted to share this moment with you."

Of course, you don't have to limit yourself to printed and mailed invitations. Email is another great option. A quick way to create an attractive email invitation is to format it in a word processor like Microsoft Word and then copy and paste it into the body of a blank email message. Assuming your mail software is set up to send messages in HTML or RTF format, the design and graphics should be retained. (If in doubt, email the invitation to yourself as a test.)

The Question of Gifts

People attending Eagle courts of honor often wonder if they're supposed to bring a gift. While traditions vary among troops, I don't think court-of-honor guests should feel obligated to come with present in hand. Some people will choose to bring gifts, of course, especially family members and close friends, and they may turn to you for advice on what to bring.

A good place to start looking for gift ideas is the BSA catalog. Over the last decade or so, the BSA has greatly expanded the range and quality of the gifts and recognition items it sells. At this writing, you could buy gifts through the BSA catalog ranging from a few dollars to more than $300. (Note that some of the more expensive gift items ship directly from the manufacturer and can take up to six weeks for delivery.)

But you don't have to limit your search to the BSA catalog. You can find plenty of bald-eagle cards, prints, and statuettes at many gift shops.

Another option, assuming the honoree is on board, is to request that gifts go to the organization his Eagle project benefited (canned goods to the soup kitchen he served, for example). Just include this request in your invitations.

Another great option – especially for troop members – is to create an event on Facebook. Among other things, this lets you include a map and take RSVPs. Just be sure to compare the Facebook RSVP list with any offline lists you're maintaining.

Developing the Ceremony

Your next big job is to develop the ceremony to be used. You may want to start with one of the samples in Chapter 7 and modify it to fit the Scout you're honoring. Your initial meeting with the Scout and his family should have given you some ideas for customizing the ceremony.

As you write the ceremony, think about the location you're planning to use: Will the action take place on a stage? Can you dim the lights for your slideshow? Where will the honoree sit?

Once you've developed your script, begin assigning parts. Some assignments will be easy: the Scoutmaster will probably do the actual badge presentation, and the Scout's religious leader or youth pastor is a good choice for the invocation and benediction. Other parts will take some thought: Who's the right person to deliver the Eagle charge, for example? Remember to use any special people the family requested.

Also remember that this is a troop function. You don't need a bunch of VIPs (Scouting or otherwise) on the program to have an effective ceremony. The new Eagle Scout *is* the VIP.

How many presenters should be involved? Six to eight main presenters is probably the maximum. The more presenters you have, the

---

Maintaining the Element of Surprise

In many troops, the honoree and his family are intimately involved in planning the ceremony. That's fine, but it poses a dilemma: How can you make the ceremony feel fresh to them? The best way is to not give them a complete, word-for-word copy of the script ahead of time. By leaving out the text of the Eagle charge, for example, you'll leave them something to look forward to.

Incidentally, a thoughtful gift for the honoree is a copy of the final script – not a dog-eared copy you pull off the lectern after the ceremony, but a fresh copy printed on nice paper and slipped into a presentation folder. This copy should be as complete as possible.

more complicated the event will be and the more time you'll waste with introductions, entrances, and exits. Your presenters may be Scouts, Scout leaders, or other adults.

Chapter 3 covers the ceremony itself in much greater detail.

Recruiting

I said earlier that the way to eat an elephant is one bite at a time. But there's actually a better way: get a lot of friends to help you. That's where recruiting comes in.

Once you've decided who you want to involve in the court of honor, you need to go out and recruit those people. Do this early to be sure that you get the people you want. As soon as they're recruited, send them a printed script with their parts highlighted.

At the same time, you need to recruit some important support people. Support jobs include physical arrangements, publicity, decorations, refreshments, the printed program, and photography/videography. You may also want to recruit someone to solicit congratulatory letters from public officials and other dignitaries. (This is usually a separate job from sending invitations.) Support functions are discussed in Chapter 8.

Shopping Spree

Part of the court of honor involves giving the new Eagle (and his parents) a number of recognition items. These usually include the Eagle badge itself, the Eagle certificate, a letter from the Chief Scout Executive, an

---

Script Tips

Here are a few tips for making printed scripts easier to work with: Before you print copies, increase the font size so that the text is legible from a distance; 16-point type seems to work well. Number all the pages in case they get mixed up. After you print your scripts, go through each presenter's copy and highlight his name each time it appears so his lines are easy to spot. Finally, paper-clip – instead of stapling – each script copy. This allows each presenter to unclip his script at the lectern and slide pages out of the way instead of noisily flipping them over.

Eagle mother's pin, and an Eagle lapel pin for the father. The certificate and letter are automatically sent by the national office in the Eagle packet; the other items are purchased from your local Scout Shop.

In addition, many troops and chartered organizations give a gift, like a plaque or a neckerchief, to the Scout. One troop I know of gives each new Eagle a flag that flew over the U.S. Capitol on his board of review date. (For details, contact your U.S. representative or one of your U.S. Senators or visit **www.usflag.org**.) Another idea is to present him with a framed Scouting print or bald-eagle photo; have troop members and court-of-honor guests write notes on the back (or the mat) to create a real treasure.

Some troops also have a large plaque in their meeting place on which they engrave the names of all their Eagle Scouts; you can purchase these and other plaques from your local Scout Shop. Be sure to allow time for engraving any plaques that you're using.

Another "item" that's often purchased is a membership in the National Eagle Scout Association (NESA); a life membership makes an especially nice gift. At this writing, regular, five-year memberships cost $35, while life memberships cost $250. However, new Eagle Scouts can join NESA for just $20 if they apply within six months of their boards of review; this special membership is good until age 23. An application comes with the Eagle packet; you can also download a copy from the NESA website. Sometimes the family has the NESA and Eagle Scout certificates framed before the court of honor. (For more information, write to NESA, 1325 W. Walnut Hill Lane, P.O. Box 152079, Irving, TX 75015-2079 or visit **www.nesa.org**.)

Your refreshment coordinator will need to order a cake and buy cups, plates, napkins, and utensils. Many of these supplies can be purchased from your local Scout Shop, where you can also buy Eagle Scout program covers.

You should visit the Scout Shop as early as possible in case some of the things you need must be ordered. The shop may keep a small supply of program covers on hand, for example, or may only stock one style. Also, some gift items must be order direct from the manufacturer, which can take several weeks. You can also order directly from the BSA catalog or website (**www.scoutstuff.org**); be sure to allow time for delivery.

An Eagle court of honor can be an expensive affair, but it doesn't have to be. You could, for example, use red, white, and blue napkins, plates, and balloons instead of the more expensive Eagle-logo items. (A good time to stock up is around Independence Day.)

Expensive or not, decide up front who is going to pay for what. For example, the family could pay for the invitations, the reception, and the NESA membership, the chartered organization could pay for the plaque, and the troop could pay for the program covers, Eagle badge, and other recognition items. Some troops will reimburse the family up to $50 or $100 for any expenses they incur. Whatever arrangements you make should be consistent from one court of honor to the next, and whatever costs the troop is expected to bear should be included in the troop budget. This approach ensures that every Scout gets a decent ceremony without precluding families from spending more if they want to.

Final Details

If the people you've recruited are doing their jobs, you should have little to do in the days before the court of honor. Your main task will be to make sure all the parts come together.

A few phone calls near the end will make a big difference. Call all your presenters to make sure they're ready. Call the custodian to make sure the building will be open. Call the senior patrol leader and have him remind all the Scouts to attend. Call everyone who's supposed to bring something (cake, programs, flags, etc.) to make sure they haven't forgotten.

A few days before the ceremony – perhaps at the end of a troop meeting – gather as many participants as possible for a quick rehearsal in the room where the ceremony will take place. Having a rehearsal will help you solve such basic problems as figuring out where people are going to stand or sit, which microphones they're going to use, who's going to control the lights, etc. It'll also point out to presenters what their cues are. You don't necessarily need to have people read every line of their parts, but you might want to consider doing so to ensure that they practice their lines at least once before the ceremony!

The Big Day

Those involved in the court of honor should arrive long before the program starts. Chairs need to be set up, the room needs to be decorated, microphones and lights need to be checked, and the thermostat needs to be set. All these chores should be finished at least half an hour before the program is due to begin.

As discussed in Chapter 8, you should lay out all the awards on a table up front in the order they'll be presented. To avoid awkwardness during the ceremony, pin the Eagle medal on the Scout's uniform and then remove it. You'll be left with two small pinholes that will serve as a guide for his mother when it comes time to pin the medal on for keeps.

Follow-up

Follow-up is brief but important. Be sure to leave the room cleaner than you found it. Send thank-you notes to the people who helped you (including the custodian and the person who let you use the building). Send a press release to the local newspapers (if they didn't already publish a story).

Finally, take some time to evaluate the court of honor and make notes for the next time. Since you did such a great job this time, you'll undoubtedly be asked to plan the troop's next court of honor, too!

Chapter 3

The Ceremony Itself

The parts of the ceremony, their purpose, and how they fit together

The Ceremony Itself

We must create situations which are romantic, which live with
the boy and stir his emotions. These ceremonies, through their
appeal to the emotions, stimulate the ideals of patriotism,
moral determination, and spiritual aspiration.
　　　　　　　　—Principles of Scoutmastership, *1930*

In the introduction, I said that each court of honor should be different, that each ceremony should reflect the accomplishments and interests of the Eagle Scout himself.

At the same time, though, every ceremony should have some common elements – an opening, the presentation of the badge, the Eagle charge, a closing, etc. And in most cases, these elements should appear in the same order.

In this chapter, we'll look at a standard format for Eagle courts of honor, a framework on which you can build your ceremony. By closely following this format, you can ensure that you've covered everything you need to cover, and in an order that makes sense. The standard format looks like this:

1.　　Before the Ceremony
2.　　Opening Period
3.　　Scouting Segment
4.　　Eagle Segment
5.　　Presentation of the Eagle Badge
6.　　Closing Period
7.　　After the Ceremony

continued on page 26

Ceremony Outline

The parts of the ceremony, as discussed in this chapter, are summarized below. Times are approximate. The Scouting segment, Eagle segment, and presentation section are discussed in more detail in chapters 4, 5, and 6, respectively.

1. **Before the Ceremony**
   Displays
   Programs distributed
   Final ceremony preparation

2. **Opening Period (10 minutes)**
   Call to order and welcoming remarks
   Introductions
   Announcements
   Invocation
   Opening ceremony
   Formal opening of the court of honor

3. **Scouting Segment (10 minutes)**
   A presentation about the purpose
   and meaning of Scouting

4. **Eagle Scout Segment (10 minutes)**
   A presentation about the significance
   and history of the Eagle Scout Award

5. **Presentation of the Eagle Badge (15-20 minutes)**
   Honoree's Scouting history or personal
   statement
   The Eagle charge
   The Eagle Scout Promise
   The presentation of the Eagle badge
   The presentation of other awards

6. **Closing Period (5 minutes)**
   Closing ceremony
   Benediction
   Closing of the court of honor

7. **After the Ceremony**
   Reception
   Clean-up

Ceremonies for Multiple Recipients

The ceremony outline actually changes very little in multi-Scout courts of honor. The main difference occurs during either the Eagle segment or the presentation phase where the honorees' Scouting histories are recounted. Here, the honorees should be spotlighted one by one. You can then present the badges, pins, etc. simultaneously and read excerpts from one set of congratulatory letters. The "Late Night" script on page 118 shows how a multi-Scout ceremony can work.

In the next few pages, I'll walk you through the ceremony and explain each part. A summary of this information appears in the chart on the previous page. Later chapters include scripts for the key sections: the Scouting segment, the Eagle segment, and the presentation of the Eagle badge. Finally, Chapter 7 contains eight complete ceremony scripts.

Before the Ceremony

Just like a good troop meeting, a good court of honor actually starts before the opening. As soon as people arrive, they should be greeted and given something to do. That "something" could include signing a guestbook, looking at a display of the honoree's memorabilia (patch vests, scrapbooks, etc.), reading the printed program, or enjoying a cup of coffee. Non-troop guests who don't know anybody will especially appreciate the diversion.

A memorabilia display can do a great job of highlighting the honoree's whole Scouting career, along with his other pursuits, while giving guests something to look at before the ceremony starts. Some parents worry that they don't have enough stuff to create a display. They needn't. Combine the honoree's Cub Scout uniform, camp T-shirts, battered first Scout handbook, assorted patches, and maybe a digital picture frame, and you can easily fill a couple of eight-foot tables.

Opening Period

The opening period is a necessary evil. Its purpose is to get the meeting started and to cover some important, but often boring, housekeeping details. It also gives you time to get everyone seated, focused, and quiet. Keep the opening period short – no more than 10 minutes – and try hard to start on time.

Here's what the opening period should include: First, the master of ceremonies calls the group to order, makes a few welcoming remarks, and introduces honored guests, key troop leaders, representatives of the chartered organization, and presenters, unless they'll be introduced later.

(By the way, it really improves the flow the ceremony if the master of ceremonies introduces all the presenters up front. During the ceremony, each presenter can then call up the next presenter before he sits down.)

The master of ceremonies then makes any announcements. If you absolutely have to make announcements, go on and get them out of the way now. And remember that non-troop guests don't really care that money for next week's campout is due tonight!

Next, an invocation is offered by a minister, rabbi, or other religious leader, preferably one who represents the boy's own place of worship or the troop's chartered organization. The invocation could also be offered by the troop's chaplain or chaplain aide. I like to give guest religious leaders a copy of the script ahead of time so they understand what's going on and can echo the ceremony's theme should they so choose.

The invocation is followed by a simple but dignified opening ceremony, performed by Scouts in the troop and/or members of the troop's sister Cub Scout pack or Venturing crew. An appropriate ceremony would be the presentation of the colors followed by the Pledge of Allegiance. (If you're going to have people stand for the invocation, make sure they know to remain standing for the opening ceremony.)

Finally, the opening period closes when someone, ideally a national council representative (but more likely someone from the district or local

---

Emotional Rollercoaster

The whole Eagle ceremony should build to a single emotional peak, when the honoree is officially declared an Eagle Scout and the audience gives him a standing ovation.

As the chart shows, the opening period contributes little to the emotional build-up. The Scouting segment and Eagle segment contribute a lot more and get people in the right frame of mind for the presentation itself, when the peak is reached.

Notice that the audience doesn't stay at the peak very long. Right after the standing ovation, they'll start looking at their watches. That's why everything after the presentation must be kept brief.

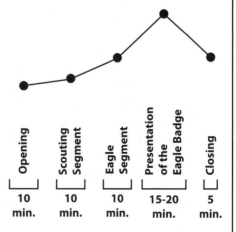

Opening	Scouting Segment	Eagle Segment	Presentation of the Eagle Badge	Closing
10 min.	10 min.	10 min.	15-20 min.	5 min.

council), formally opens the court of honor. This little ritual effectively ends the opening period and serves as a bridge to the next section. The person usually says something like, "By the power vested in me by the National Council of the Boy Scouts of America, I declare this court of honor to be duly convened for the sole purpose of presenting the Eagle Scout Award to _____."

Scouting Segment and Eagle Segment

By the end of the opening period, you should have the audience's attention. Now it's time to remind them why they're here and to make them feel good about Scouting in general and the new Eagle in particular. This happens in the Scouting and Eagle segments of the court of honor.

The Scouting segment is a brief ceremony, presentation, or speech that addresses the purpose and meaning of Scouting. Probably the most common Scouting segment is a candle ceremony in which Scouts explain the meaning of the Scout Law.

Next comes the Eagle segment, where one or more adult Eagle Scouts, district representatives, or troop leaders address the history and significance of the Eagle badge and begin to shift the focus to the honoree. An example would be "The Legend of Eagle Mountain," in which a narrator describes in general terms the Scout's climb up the Eagle trail.

Together the Scouting segment and the Eagle segment should take no more than 20 minutes. And I emphasize the word *together*; there should be a logical flow from one to the next.

A keynote speaker could be used for one of these segments, probably the Eagle segment. Some people also like to include music, perhaps a song like "Trail the Eagle," "On My Honor," "Wind Beneath my Wings," "On Eagle's Wings," "Stand by Me," or "What a Wonderful World." Such a musical interlude would probably work best at the end of the Eagle segment. Keep in mind, however, that a three- or four-minute song can seem to last an eternity if nothing's happening on the stage or on a screen. (In fact, that's why it's typically better to use music as a soundtrack for a slideshow.)

Chapters 4 and 5 give several examples for these two parts of the ceremony.

Presentation of the Eagle Badge

If the Scouting and Eagle segments were effective, you'll have the audience feeling good, perhaps a little misty-eyed, and definitely primed for the big moment. Over the next 15 to 20 minutes, their emotions will reach their high point.

Now it's time to really focus on the honoree. He's brought forward, and we hear about his Scouting career, either from him or from a Scout leader or fellow Scout. (Note that some of this may happen earlier if you use an Eagle segment like "The Trail to Eagle.")

This part of the ceremony is a good place to share fun anecdotes or show pictures that illustrate the honoree's Scouting journey. It's also a great time for a little humor, as long as it doesn't humiliate a Scout. If you go the anecdote route, consider three speakers: one representing Cub Scouting, one representing the honoree's early Boy Scout years, and one discussing his later years and/or his Eagle project. Encourage each to share one or two anecdotes – no more – from that part of his life.

After the stories are told and the pictures are shown, a presenter – ideally an older Eagle Scout who's important to the honoree – gives him a charge or challenge and that person or the Scoutmaster administers the Eagle Scout Promise.

Next, the honoree's parents are brought forward, and the formal

---

Accounting for Non-nuclear Families

The ceremonies in this book assume that the Scout has one father and one mother and that both plan to participate in the ceremony. These days, of course, many Eagles come from single-parent families or blended families. They may live with adoptive parents, stepparents, or even grandparents, and they may have a non-custodial parent who wants to participate in the court of honor.

That's no problem as long as you take the honoree's family structure into account when scripting the court of honor. If the Scout's father is deceased, you might say, "John, we wish your dad could be with us today – and we know he's with us in spirit. In his place, your uncle Fred will present the Eagle Scout certificate." If the Scout has both a father and a stepfather present, say something like, "Bill, you've been fortunate to receive fatherly advice and guidance from two men along the Eagle trail. We'd like your father to present you with the Eagle certificate and your stepfather to present the Eagle neckerchief."

You can make similar adjustments for other flavors of families.

presentation is made. The new Eagle hugs his mother and shakes his father's hand. The master of ceremonies says, "I present to you our troop's newest Eagle Scout, _____!" and the audience gives a standing ovation. (Consider asking a few people ahead of time to initiate the standing ovation.) This is the emotional high point of the entire ceremony and lets the audience release their pent-up emotion.

At this point, the family, troop, and chartered organization may want to give the honoree gifts, as described in Chapter 2. You may also want to read excerpts from some of the congratulatory letters received. (Don't read every word of every letter, especially the part where your U.S. Senator apologizes for not being able to attend the court of honor.) If he didn't get a chance earlier, the Eagle Scout may want to present his mother with flowers or his Scoutmaster with a gift.

Chapter 6 covers the presentation in more detail.

Closing Period

In terms of program and emotion, you're now on the downhill side, so the closing period needs to move along quickly. That's the reason announcements are made during the opening period.

There are a few things left to cover, though, and you have about five minutes to cover them. These things include a brief (and optional) closing ceremony by members of the troop, a benediction by whoever did the invocation, and closing remarks (little more than "Thank you and please join us at the reception.") from the master of ceremonies.

Some troops end the ceremony by having the audience stand while the honoree and his family leave first. This lets you get them in place for pictures or cake-cutting at the reception and gives the audience one more chance to applaud.

After the Ceremony

The main event after the ceremony is typically the reception. You can either set up a formal receiving line or just let people congratulate the new Eagle as they mingle and eat cake. After the necessary cleaning up, you can go home and celebrate your great success.

Chapter 4

Scouting Segments

A series of mini-ceremonies and presentations that address the purpose and meaning of Scouting

Scouting Segments

The ceremonies should be based upon the ideals of the
Scout Oath and Law and be conducted on a high plane
so as to inspire the boy with the greatness of our movement.
—Handbook for Scoutmasters, *1938*

The Scouting segment of the program, which follows the opening, focuses on the meaning of Scouting. This chapter includes 12 appropriate Scouting segments, which are also available for download from **www .eaglebook.com/scripts/**.

Keep in mind that the Scouting segment you select will be followed by an Eagle segment. The two segments should complement each other and not be contradictory or redundant.

1. Scout Law Candle Ceremony

This ceremony has been around since at least the 1930s, but it can still be effective if it's done well. You'll need a candelabrum with 12 candles, representing the points of the Scout Law, along with a 13th candle, representing the Spirit of Scouting. (See the examples on page 166.) A Scout stands behind each of the Scout Law candles. Each Scout's part is printed on a card and laid on the table in front of him.

Depending on the personnel you have available, you can assign each Scout to one, two, or three candles. You can also add Cub Scouts, Varsity Scouts, Venturers, or Sea Scouts to the mix, which is especially appropriate if the honoree has been involved in those programs.

Most people use the text from the Boy Scout Handbook. *In the twelfth edition, you would use the text on pages 24-25. In the eleventh edition, refer to pages 47-54.*

For the sake of variety and historical interest, the text reproduced here comes from the 1918 Handbook for Boys. *You can also develop your own text – or even have the new Eagle Scout write his own definition of each point of the Law.*

Leader *(holding lighted "Spirit" candle)*: This candle represents the Spirit of Scouting, a spirit which burns brightly in the heart of every Scout. Let us renew our spirit by reminding ourselves of the meaning of the Scout Law.

(He hands the candle to the first Scout. As this Scout reads his part, he lights the candle in front of him. When he has finished, he hands the candle to the next Scout. Continue in this manner until all 12 Scouts have finished.)

First Scout: A Scout is trustworthy. A Scout's honor is to be trusted. If he were to violate his honor by telling a lie, or by cheating, or by not doing exactly a given task, when trusted on his honor, he may be directed to hand over his Scout badge.

Second Scout: A Scout is loyal. He is loyal to all to whom loyalty is due: his Scout leader, his home, and parents and country.

Third Scout: A Scout is helpful. He must be prepared at any time to save life, help injured persons, and share the home duties. He must do at least one good turn to somebody every day.

Fourth Scout: A Scout is friendly. He is a friend to all and a brother to every other Scout.

Fifth Scout: A Scout is courteous. He is polite to all, especially to women, children, old people, and the weak and helpless. He must not take pay for being helpful or courteous.

Sixth Scout: A Scout is kind. He is a friend to animals. He will not kill nor hurt any living creature needlessly, but will strive to save and protect all harmless life.

Seventh Scout: A Scout is obedient. He obeys his parents, Scoutmaster, patrol leader, and all other duly constituted authorities.

Eighth Scout: A Scout is cheerful. He smiles whenever he can. His obedience to orders is prompt and cheery. He never shirks nor grumbles at hardships.

Ninth Scout: A Scout is thrifty. He does not wantonly destroy property. He works faithfully, wastes nothing, and makes the best use of his opportunities. He saves his money so that he may pay his own way, be generous to those in need, and helpful to worthy objects. He may work for pay, but must not receive tips for courtesies or good turns.

Tenth Scout: A Scout is brave. He has the courage to face danger in spite of fear, and to stand up for the right against the coaxing of friends or the jeers or threats of enemies, and defeat does not down him.

Eleventh Scout: A Scout is clean. He keeps clean in body and thought, stands for clean speech, clean sport, clean habits, and travels with a clean crowd.

Twelfth Scout: A Scout is reverent. He is reverent toward God. He is faithful in his religious duties, and respects the convictions of others in matters of custom and religion.

(The last Scout blows out the "Spirit" candle. The Scouts then return to their seats.)

2. John Wayne's Scout Law

I like this explanation of the Scout Law – although you may have to explain to your Scouts who John Wayne was!

There are several ways to use this text. You can present it like the Scout Law candle ceremony on page 32, have a single person read it, or have one person say the points of the Law and another read the explanations. In the latter case, have the first reader stand at the lectern; have the second reader stand at attention and make the Scout sign as he recites his part.

First Reader: "A Scout is trustworthy, loyal, helpful, friendly, courteous, kind, obedient, cheerful, thrifty, brave, clean, and reverent." Nice words. Trouble is, we learn them so young we sometimes don't get all the understanding that goes with them. I take care of that in my family. As each boy reaches Scout age I make sure he learns the Scout Law. Then I break it down for him with a few things I've picked up in the more than half a century since I learned it.

Second Reader: A Scout is trustworthy.

First Reader: The badge of honesty. Having it lets you look any man straight in the eye. Lacking it, he won't look back. Keep it at the top of your list.

Second Reader: A Scout is loyal.

First Reader: The very word is life itself, for without loyalty we have no love of person or country.

Second Reader: A Scout is helpful.

First Reader: Part sharing, part caring. By helping each other, we help ourselves, not to mention mankind. Be always full of help – the dying man's last word.

Second Reader: A Scout is friendly.

First Reader: Brotherhood is part of that word. You can take it in a lot of directions – and do – but make sure and start with brotherhood.

Second Reader: A Scout is courteous.

First Reader: Allow each person his human dignity, which means a lot more than saying "Yes, ma'am" and "Thank you, sir." It reflects an attitude that later in life you "wish you honored more ... earlier in life." Save yourself that problem. Do it now.

Second Reader: A Scout is kind.

First Reader: This one word would stop wars and erase hatreds. But it's like your bicycle. It's just no good unless you get out and use it.

Second Reader: A Scout is obedient.

First Reader: Start at home, practice it on your family, enlarge it to your friends, share it with humanity.

Second Reader: A Scout is cheerful.

First Reader: Anyone can put on a happy face when the going's good. The secret is to wear it as a mask for your problems. It might surprise you how many others do the same thing.

Second Reader: A Scout is thrifty.

First Reader: Means a lot more than putting pennies away, and it's the opposite of cheap. Common sense covers it just about as well as anything.

Second Reader: A Scout is brave.

First Reader: You don't have to fight to be brave. Millions of good, fine, decent folks show more bravery than heavyweight champs just by getting out of bed every morning, going out to do a good day's work, and living the best life they know how against a lot of odds. Brave. Keep the word handy every day of your life.

Second Reader: A Scout is clean.

First Reader: Soap and water help a lot on the outside. But it's the inside that counts, and don't you ever forget it.

Second Reader: A Scout is reverent.

First Reader: Believe in anything you want to believe in, but keep God at the top of it. With Him, life can be a beautiful experience. Without Him, you're just biding time.

3. George Washington's Scout Law

Here's another interesting interpretation of the Scout Law, using the words of someone who died more than a century before the Scout Law was created. See "John Wayne's Scout Law" on page 34 for tips on using this text.

First Reader: Few U.S. presidents have embodied the Scout Law more than the first, George Washington, even though he died long before Scouting began. At age 15, Washington created a set of rules for himself, many of which align with points of the Scout Law. Listen to the wisdom of President Washington.

Second Reader: A Scout is trustworthy.

First Reader: Undertake not what you cannot perform, but be careful to keep your promise.

Second Reader: A Scout is loyal.

First Reader: Be not hasty to believe flying reports to the disparagement of any. Speak not evil of the absent, for it is unjust.

Second Reader: A Scout is helpful.

First Reader: Wherein you reprove another be unblamable yourself, for example is more prevalent than precepts. In visiting the sick do not play the physician, if you be not knowing therein.

Second Reader: A Scout is friendly.

First Reader: Show not yourself glad at the misfortune of another, though he were your enemy. Let your conversation be without malice or envy.

Second Reader: A Scout is courteous.

First Reader: Be not forward, but friendly and courteous, the first to salute, hear, and answer. Speak not when others speak, sit not when others stand, speak not when you should hold your peace, walk not when others stop, turn not your back to others, especially in speaking; lean not on anyone.

Second Reader: A Scout is kind.

First Reader: When a man does all he can, though it succeeds not well, blame not him that did it.

Second Reader: A Scout is obedient.

First Reader: Honor and obey your natural parents although they be poor. Strive not with your superiors in argument, but always submit your judgment to others with modesty.

Second Reader: A Scout is cheerful.

First Reader: Speak not of doleful things in times of mirth; nor at the table; put on a cheerful countenance, for good humor makes one dish of meat a feast.

Second Reader: A Scout is thrifty.

First Reader: Let your discourse with men of business be short and comprehensive. In your apparel be modest, and endeavor to accommodate nature rather than to procure admiration.

Second Reader: A Scout is brave.

First Reader: Fight to keep alive in your breast that little spark of celestial fire called conscience.

Second Reader: A Scout is clean.

First Reader: Use no reproachful language against anyone, neither curse nor revile. Let your recreations be manful, not sinful.

Second Reader: A Scout is reverent.

First Reader: When you speak of God, or His attributes, let it be seriously in reverence.

4. The Scout Law in Scripture

The words in this Scouting segment come directly from the Bible, making it appropriate for a Christian-themed ceremony. (If your honoree comes from another faith tradition, you may be able to create something similar with a little help from his religious leaders.) See "John Wayne's Scout Law" on page 34 for tips on using this text.

First Reader: Robert Baden-Powell, the founder of Scouting, once said, "There is no religious side to the movement; the whole of it is based on religion, that is on the realization and service of God." In keeping with that spirit, let's consider how the Scout Law aligns with Scripture.

Second Reader: A Scout is trustworthy.

First Reader: You shall not give false testimony against your neighbor – Exodus 20:16.

Second Reader: A Scout is loyal.

First Reader: Whoever can be trusted with very little can also be trusted with much, and whoever is dishonest with very little will also be dishonest with much. – Luke 16:10

Second Reader: A Scout is helpful.

First Reader: There will always be poor people in the land. Therefore I command you to be openhanded toward your fellow Israelites who are poor and needy in your land. – Deuteronomy 15:11

Second Reader: A Scout is friendly.

First Reader: How good and pleasant it is when God's people live together in unity! – Psalm 133:1

Second Reader: A Scout is courteous.

First Reader: Do not let any unwholesome talk come out of your mouths, but only what is helpful for building others up according to their needs, that it may benefit those who listen. – Ephesians 4:29

Second Reader: A Scout is kind.

First Reader: The righteous care for the needs of their animals, but the kindest acts of the wicked are cruel. – Proverbs 12:10

Second Reader: A Scout is obedient.

First Reader: Children, obey your parents in the Lord, for this is right. "Honor your father and mother" – which is the first commandment with a promise – "so that it may go well with you and that you may enjoy long life on the earth." – Ephesians 6:1-3

Second Reader: A Scout is cheerful.

First Reader: A happy heart makes the face cheerful, but heartache crushes the spirit. – Proverbs 15:13

Second Reader: A Scout is thrifty.

First Reader: Go to the ant, you sluggard; consider its ways and be wise! It has no commander, no overseer or ruler, yet it stores its provisions in summer and gathers its food at harvest. – Proverbs 6:6-8

Second Reader: A Scout is brave.

First Reader: Be strong and courageous. Do not be afraid or terrified because of them, for the Lord your God goes with you; he will never leave you nor forsake you. – Deuteronomy 31:6

Second Reader: A Scout is clean.

First Reader: Who may ascend the mountain of the Lord? Who may stand in his holy place? The one who has clean hands and a pure heart, who does not trust in an idol or swear by a false god. – Psalm 24:3-4

Second Reader: A Scout is reverent.

First Reader: Love the Lord your God with all your heart and with all your soul and with all your mind and with all your strength. – Mark 12:30

5. The Development of the Scout Law

This piece is rather long but quite interesting. It is designed to be read by five people, as shown. You may end it by having the fifth reader recite the Scout Law or by having all Scouts and Scouters stand and rededicate themselves to following the Scout Law.

First Reader: One of the oldest surviving set of rules for how men should behave comes to us from the ancient Greeks. In the third century B.C., young men of 17 took the following oath to become citizens of Athens:

> We will never bring disgrace on this, our city, by an act of dishonesty or cowardice.
> We will fight for the ideals and sacred things of the city both alone and with many.
> We will revere and obey the city's laws, and will do our best to incite a like reverence and respect in those above us who are prone to annul them or set them at naught.
> We will strive increasingly to quicken the public's sense of civic duty.
> Thus in all these ways we will transmit this city, not only not less, but greater, better, and more beautiful than it was transmitted to us.

Second Reader: With the growth of modern religions, another, simpler idea of how men should behave developed. Referred to as the Golden Rule, it is taught by religions as diverse as Christianity, Judaism, Buddhism, and Brahmanism. Christianity's version is found in Matthew 7:12: "So in everything, do to others what you would have them do to you, for this sums up the Law and the Prophets."

Third Reader: During the Middle Ages, the code of chivalry was developed to teach knights how they should behave. One form of this code read as follows:

> Be always ready with your armor on, except when you are taking your rest at night.
> Defend the poor, and help them that cannot defend themselves.
> Do nothing to hurt or offend anyone else.
> Be prepared to fight in the defense of your country.
> At whatever you are working, try to win honor and a name for honesty.
> Never break your promise.
> Maintain the honor of your country with your life.
> Rather die honest than live shamelessly.
> Chivalry requires that youth should be trained to perform the most laborious and humble offices with cheerfulness and grace; and to do good unto others.

Fourth Reader: In the early years of the twentieth century, a man named Robert Stephenson Smyth Baden-Powell took all these codes of conduct for men and turned them into a code of conduct for boys. His Scout Law, as he called it, read as follows:

> A Scout's honor is to be trusted.
> A Scout is loyal to the king, and to his officers, and to his country, and to his employers.
> A Scout's duty is to be useful and to help others.
> A Scout is a friend to all, and a brother to every other Scout, no matter to what social class the other belongs.
> A Scout is courteous.
> A Scout is a friend to animals.

A Scout obeys orders of his patrol leader or Scoutmaster without question.
A Scout smiles and whistles under all circumstances.
A Scout is thrifty.

Fifth Reader: A few years later, Baden-Powell's program and ideas crossed the Atlantic Ocean. With the founding of the Boy Scouts of America, B-P's Scout Law was turned into a code that more than 90 million boys have learned and lived by. A Scout is trustworthy, loyal, helpful, friendly, courteous, kind, obedient, cheerful, thrifty, brave, clean, and reverent.

6. Scout Oath Rededication

A favorite Scouting ceremony is the Scout Oath rededication. Sometimes the Scout Oath rededication is combined with the Scout Law candle ceremony described on page 32.

This ceremony is simple. Have all Scouts and Scouters stand, make the Scout sign, and repeat the Scout Oath together. It can easily be turned into a candle ceremony if you have a candelabrum that holds three candles. Using a candle representing the Spirit of Scouting, light a candle as each part of the Scout Oath (duty to God and country, duty to others, duty to self) is repeated.

7. What the Scout Oath Means to Me

This piece gives a Scout's-eye view of the Scout Oath. Written by Scout David McGrath, it was inspired by Red Skelton's recitation of the Pledge of Allegiance as explained to him by a boyhood teacher.

Use two Scouts for this presentation. The first stands at attention making the Scout sign; the other stands at the lectern.

You may want to end with a Scout Oath rededication.

First Scout: On my honor.

Second Scout: Meaning your solemn promise; a promise that relies on your good reputation as to whether or not it will be carried out.

First Scout: I will do my best.

Second Scout: Your best? What is it? It's giving it all you've got when you've got something to do – and working on it with all your heart and soul and mind, all the strength and devotion you've got. Then you're doing your best.

First Scout: To do my duty.

Second Scout: To do the job; to meet the responsibilities; to do what has to be done – not just halfway, not just half a job, but completely – completely and fully so that you're proud of your work.

First Scout: To God and my country.

Second Scout: Duty to whom? First, to God. Fulfill your religious responsibilities; uphold your religious beliefs. Second, to your country. I know you've been told how lucky you are to live in a free country. I hope that you are aware of it. Being told and being aware are two different things. And I hope that you will soon be aware of the responsibility you have to your country – your duty.

First Scout: To obey the Scout Law.

Second Scout: Meaning to obey it, to follow it completely, not just halfway. And not just the first six points or the last three or every other one, but all twelve points, at all times.

First Scout: To help other people at all times.

Second Scout: To help ... it doesn't say much. It could mean saving a life or changing a tire or carrying a bag of groceries. To help other people, not just your family. And at all times, not just when it is convenient for you or when your Scoutmaster is watching – but at all times. And the best time is when you have to go out of your way to do it.

First Scout: To keep myself physically strong.

Second Scout: Just what it says – physically strong; ready to defend yourself, your Scouting principles, your country.

First Scout: Mentally awake.

Second Scout: Keep alert, observing, always trying to learn.

First Scout: And morally straight.

Second Scout: In thought and actions, decide what is right and what is wrong and stand by the right.

So there you have it. And the next time you recite the Scout Oath, don't just say it as something you've memorized, but say it as something you mean.

8. The Four Great Scout Duties

The third edition of the Handbook for Boys, *published during the 1930s, described the four "great duties" of Scouts. This presentation is adapted from that text.*
Use five readers for this presentation. Consider following up with a Scout Oath rededication.

First Scout: The Scout Oath is a very clear statement of good citizenship. In it are the four great duties of life: duty to God, duty to country, duty to others, and duty to self. Duties are the foundation of all fair dealing. Every privilege in the world rests upon an equal responsibility. For everything we receive, there are things we must give.

As we try to do our best to live the Scout Oath, let us think about these duties:

Second Scout: Duty to God. What is a Scout's duty to God? What does a Scout owe to the Infinite Creator of the universe, the source of life itself?

Belief in God? Of course. Obedience to his basic commandments and the larger commandment to brotherhood? Of course – but more than these, the real man keeps himself in conscious harmony with God and with God's other creatures, his fellow man, and in active participation with his church, synagogue, mosque, or other place of worship.

In doing their duty to God, Scouts extend to other faiths the same courtesy and consideration and respect that they expect for their own.

Third Scout: Duty to country. What is a Scout's duty to his country? What does he owe to the land which gives him free education, things to enjoy and do, and also the chance to be what he wants to be?

To obey her laws? Yes. To respect her institutions? Yes – but more, to as willingly live for America as thousands of patriots have been eager to die for America. To die for one's country calls for supreme courage – but to live right, to work, to produce, to help, to save, to obey the nation's laws, to live the Scout Law day after day in little things calls for just as much courage spread over a longer time.

Fourth Scout: Duty to others. What is a Scout's duty to other people? What do they have a right to expect of a Scout?

That he shall be friendly? Yes – all good citizens expect that from each other. That he shall be fair? Yes, of course – but more than that, people know that the Scout promise to do a good turn daily means that, like the ancient knight, the Scout helps others as he would want them to help him. But he does it with no thought of return, just for the pleasure of doing it as a good citizen.

Fifth Scout: Duty to self. What is a Scout's duty to himself? What does he owe to the immortal personality that he is?

He needs to grow – in stature, in strength, in knowledge and wisdom, in favor with God and man – to grow into greater value and useful-ness and skill. The last words of the Scout Oath clearly point to a balanced duty to self: "Keep myself physically strong, mentally awake, and morally straight." Only when he does that can he have the full measure of fun, happiness, and joy from living.

9. Scouting's Codes of Conduct

This piece, as you will see, ties in neatly with the Eagle Scout Promise that's designed to be part of the presentation of the Eagle award. It's most appropriate if the honoree was a Cub Scout. Leave out the Venturing section if it doesn't apply.

The Scouting program is designed to grow with the boy. Tiger Cub activities, for example, are quite simple when compared with those of a Boy Scout troop. And we require much more of Boy Scouts than we do of Tiger Cubs.

Tiger Cubs, in case you've forgotten, are first-grade Cub Scouts. Like their older brothers, one of the first things they do is learn the Cub Scout promise:

> I, *(name)*, promise to do my best
> To do my duty to God and my country,
> To help other people, and
> To obey the Law of the Pack.

The Law reads as follows:

> The Cub Scout follows Akela.
> The Cub Scout helps the pack go.
> The pack helps the Cub Scout grow.
> The Cub Scout gives goodwill.

The motto of the Cub Scouts is "Do Your Best."

The next step, of course, is Boy Scouting, where boys learn the Oath and the Law that we say at each of our meetings. Boy Scouting also has a motto – "Be Prepared" – and a slogan – "Do a Good Turn Daily."

Many Scouts, like our honoree, go on to participate in Venturing, Scouting's program for older youths. Venturers recite their own solemn oath:

As a Venturer, I promise to do my duty to God and help strengthen America, to help others, and to seek truth, fairness, and adventure in our world.

Venturers also live by a unique code:

As a Venturer, I believe that America's strength lies in our trust in God and in the courage, strength, and traditions of our people.

I will, therefore, be faithful in my religious duties and will maintain a personal sense of honor in my own life.

I will treasure my American heritage and will do all I can to preserve and enrich it.

I will recognize the dignity and worth of all humanity and will use fair play and goodwill in my daily life.

I will acquire the Venturing attitude that seeks the truth in all things and adventure on the frontiers of our changing world.

During his Scouting career, our honoree has learned and striven to obey all these promises, oaths, laws, mottoes, and slogans. Later tonight, he will repeat one more promise, the Eagle Scout Promise. The important thing to remember – and this applies to all of us – is that we shouldn't forget the promises we've made before just because we're making a new promise now. It's still important to do our best, to help other people, to follow Akela and give goodwill, to be prepared, and to do a good turn daily.

The Scout Oath, the Scout Law, and all the rest are not just for Scouts; they're for life.

10. The Four Winds

This Scouting segment is used in the "Order of the Arrow" script on page 111. However, you could use it in virtually any Eagle court of honor. It's a powerful way to present the meaning behind the ideals of Scouting.

The Four Winds stand at the north, south, east, and west corners of the room; the leader stands at the microphone. At the front of the room is a candelabrum with 12 candles, representing the points of the Scout Law. As each of the Four Winds recites a point of the Scout Law, a uniformed Scout lights a candle.

Leader: As Scouts, we are bound together in brotherhood by the Scout Law, a sacred set of principles for living whose origins are lost in the mist of time. Listen now to the wisdom of the winds.

East Wind: I am the spirit of the East Wind. I represent the common law, a Scout's duty to God and to country. Trustworthy, loyal, and helpful are the qualities that a man must possess who lives by the laws of this land. The Scout must be always worthy of his brother's trust and show loyalty to all to whom it is due. May the daily good turn be a central focus of your life.

West Wind: As the spirit of the West Wind, I represent the law of equity, your duty to country and to others. Friendly, courteous, and kind are the principles that speak of conscience. They create the atmosphere that comes from within your heart. Kindle the desire to be a friend to those of all ages and stations in life. Be courteous to those whom you pass along the trail. Cast away the harmful spirits of unfriendliness and selfishness.

South Wind: I am the spirit of the South Wind. I represent civil law, your duty to others and to self. Obedient, cheerful, and thrifty are the marks of civility. Obedience is something we all must learn, to take orders and carry them out cheerfully. Real thrift means spending both money and time wisely and sharing both with those less fortunate than us.

North Wind: I am the spirit of the North Wind, the most powerful of all. I represent the divine law, your duty to be brave and clean and reverent. To be brave is to be unselfish in service, always prepared to face the unknown. Cast from your mind and body any unclean spirits that try to weaken or destroy you. Live a life of reverence toward God.

11. One Hundred Scouts

The statistics in the following piece are impressive and make a good lead-in to talking about the honoree himself. I think this piece is especially appropriate for a 17- or 18-year-old Eagle Scout or one who already falls into one of the categories described.

I don't know where these statistics originally came from – and I doubt they're all still accurate – but it's a good piece anyway.

Of any 100 boys who become Scouts, it must be confessed that 30 will drop out in their first year. Perhaps this may be regarded as a failure, but in later life all of these will remember that they had been Scouts and will speak well of the program.

Of the 100, only rarely will one ever appear before a juvenile court judge. Twelve of the 100 will be from families who have no religious affiliation. Through Scouting, these 12 and many of their families will be brought into contact with a church, synagogue, or mosque, and will continue to be active all their lives. Six of the 100 will enter the ministry.

Each of the 100 will learn something from Scouting. Almost all will develop hobbies that will add interest throughout the rest of their lives. Many will serve in the military and in varying degrees profit from their Scout training. At least one will use it to save another person's life, and many will credit it with saving their own.

Five of the 100 will reach the rank of Eagle, and at least one will later say that he values his Eagle badge above his college degree. Many will find their future vocation through merit-badge work and Scouting contacts. Seventeen of the 100 boys will later become Scout leaders and will give leadership to thousands of additional boys.

Only one in four boys in America will become a Scout, but it is interesting to know that of the leaders of this nation in business, religion, and politics, three out of four were Scouts.

Tonight we honor one Scout in a hundred. We know the things he has done in the past; imagine what he will do in the future.

12. Scouting's Bottom Line

This Scouting segment is based in part on a 2005 research study, "Values of Americans: A Study of Ethics and Character," that Harris Interactive conducted on behalf of the Boy Scouts of America. You may want to update the list of Eagle Scouts or supplement it with the names of well-known Eagle Scouts in your community.

Folks who don't know any better think Boy Scouts spend all their time building fires and earning badges. But Scouting is really about building character and learning life skills. So how well does the program work?

Amazingly well.

A few years ago, Harris Interactive conducted a study for the Boy Scouts of America. It found that the vast majority of men who'd been Scouts for at least five years believe Scouting taught them some pretty important values: To always tell the truth. To be a team player. To take care of the environment. To respect the life and property of others. To take pride in America. To respect the elderly. And to have confidence in their own abilities.

In fact, 99 percent of these long-term Scouts said Scouting helps build character – 99 percent. (Perhaps the other one percent didn't understand the question.)

The Harris survey found many tangible benefits to being in Scouting. Former Scouts are more likely to own their own homes, more likely to graduate from college, and more likely to earn high salaries. They're more likely to attend religious services every week, more likely to vote in every election, and more likely to support charities.

They're also more likely to become leaders. Just consider some of the men who've achieved Scouting's highest rank over the years: Hank Aaron, Neil Armstrong, Stephen Breyer, Gerald Ford, Steve Fossett, Robert Gates, J.W. Marriott Jr., Steven Spielberg, and Sam Walton.

We know what those men accomplished after becoming Eagle Scouts. We can only imagine what our honoree will accomplish in the years to come.

Chapter 5

Eagle Segments

A series of mini-ceremonies and presentations that address the history and significance of the Eagle Scout Award

Eagle Segments

*The Eagle Scout badge stands for a job started
by a boy when he first joined Scouting – a job
started and finished.*

—Troop Activities, *1962*

The Eagle segment of the court of honor relates directly to the Eagle
Scout Award and often to the honoree himself. The nine segments in this
chapter (which are also available for download from **www.eaglebook
.com/scripts/**) remind us of what it means to be an Eagle Scout and
what one has to do to earn Boy Scouting's highest rank.

1. The Legend of Eagle Mountain

*I wrote this piece several years ago as the script to a slideshow I used to open
a court of honor. If you have the resources, you may want to assemble your
own show to go along with this text. Try interspersing mountain scenes with
pictures of the honoree as he's grown up in the Scouting program.*

*With the advent of computer projectors, color scanners, and presentation
software like Microsoft PowerPoint, you can create an electronic slideshow
instead of relying on 35mm slides. Going the high-tech route saves money and
gives you increased flexibility in your presentation. For example, you can add
transition effects between slides or add text to your pictures. The possibilities are
really unlimited.*

Early one morning a young boy stood at a trailhead. Before him rose
a mighty mountain, which seemed all the mightier when compared with
his smallness.

A trail led to the mountain and then up it to incredible heights before vanishing in the clouds. On this trail the boy could see other boys and young men, some of whom turned and beckoned him to follow.

The boy began to climb, refusing perhaps to believe that he could ever reach the top. At first the trail rose gently, and the boy had many companions. But soon he began to sweat and breathe heavily, and many of his companions turned away. And still the boy climbed.

At times he climbed quickly. At times he climbed slowly. At times he had to go down a little way to find another path or stop a while to catch his breath. But still he climbed. The trail became steeper, the air thinner, but the climber scarcely noticed for he had, along the way, become stronger of body and hardier of spirit. And still he climbed.

And finally in the cool peace of eveningtime, he stood alone at the top of the world and looked around him. To the left he saw a fiery golden sunset. To the right he saw a diamond-studded, silky-black night sky. Behind him he saw the trail that he had followed and the hikers who were following in his footsteps.

And in front of him he saw another mountain. And another. And another. And a whole procession of mountains marching off to the horizon. But the young man (for now he *was* a man) knew that none of these other mountains was insurmountable, that all could and would be climbed. For he had learned many skills in the climbing of the first mountain, and he would carry those skills with him long after this mountain was forgotten.

And besides, he could begin climbing the next mountain tomorrow. Tonight he would rest and celebrate and ponder the journey that he had completed. And so tonight, we pause to rest and celebrate and honor this fine young man, Eagle Scout _____, as he stands at the top of the world and looks around him.

2. The Requirements of an Eagle Scout

Some of the people in the audience at the court of honor won't really know what it means to be an Eagle Scout. This piece should help them understand. It outlines many of the 325 or so requirements the Eagle Scout has completed.

The requirements described here all come from Tenderfoot, Second Class, First Class, and the Eagle-required merit badges. Depending on which options the Scout took in a couple of areas (such as choosing Hiking or Cycling instead of Swimming), he may have done slightly different things.

We are here tonight to honor a young man as he becomes an Eagle Scout. As we do so, it's important to reflect on what it means to be an Eagle Scout.

The 1938 *Handbook for Scoutmasters* put it this way:

> The badges which accompany his advancement and which the Scout wears on his Uniform are not to show that he has "passed certain tests." There should be no past tense implied! On the contrary, each badge cries out "I can, right now and here!"

So what can the Eagle Scout do? Let's take a look at some of the things he has done in preparing to be an Eagle Scout.

In terms of badges, he has earned the Scout badge and the ranks of Tenderfoot, Second Class, First Class, Star, Life, and finally Eagle. Along the way, he earned 12 required merit badges and nine elective merit badges, served in troop leadership positions for a total of 16 months, and spent at least 13 hours on service projects, not including the many hours he spent on his Eagle Scout service project. In all, he has completed approximately 325 different requirements.

So what have these requirements taught him? Who *is* the Eagle Scout?

First and foremost, of course, he is an outdoorsman. He knows how to camp, swim, hike, use woods tools, build a fire, use a camp stove, and find his way with map and compass. He's spent at least 20 days and nights camping out in a tent he pitched on a site he selected. Many of those times he planned his own menu and cooked his own food.

The Eagle Scout is comfortable with nature. He can identify local animals and plants, including poisonous plants. He understands the causes of water, land, and air pollution and developed a project to solve an environmental problem.

He embodies the Scout motto, "Be Prepared." He knows how to treat fractures, head injuries, hypothermia, convulsions, frostbite, burns, abdominal pain, muscle cramps, even knocked-out teeth. He knows what to do in case of fire, explosion, desert emergency, motor-vehicle accident, mountain accident, food poisoning, gas leak, earthquake, flood, tornado, hurricane, atomic emergency, and avalanche.

The Eagle Scout is a good citizen. He's been to a city meeting and knows how the city government is organized. He knows who his U.S. Senators and Representative are and has written a letter to one of them about a national issue. He's read the Declaration of Independence and the U.S. Constitution.

He knows how to manage his money and understands the risks and benefits of putting his money in savings bonds, mutual funds, common stock, and real estate. He has set financial goals and worked toward achieving those goals.

The Eagle Scout has also set and worked toward fitness goals. He's competed against himself in tests of aerobic endurance, flexibility, and muscular strength. He knows what it means to be physically, mentally, and socially fit.

He's a good family member. He knows what things are important to the members of his family and has talked to his family about finances, drug abuse, and growing up.

All of these things he did in order to earn the merit badges required for Eagle. Beyond those, he earned nine elective merit badges, which introduced him to such subjects as: *(list some of the honoree's elective merit badges here)*

So what is an Eagle Scout? Well, to quote that old *Handbook for Scoutmasters* again, he is a young man "who is qualified to help others as well as take care of himself." His badge is not "a decoration, but rather a symbol of knowledge and ability."

3. The Obligations of an Eagle Scout

A common element of Eagle courts of honor describes the obligations of an Eagle Scout. The standard version is found in Troop Program Resources *and is quite good.*

I wrote the version below as an alternative. My version focuses on qualities of a good leader; the standard version focuses on aspects of good character. Both should be in your repertoire.

This piece can also be used as an Eagle charge. See page 156.

See page 177 for a lighted Eagle badge sign that you can use with this segment.

Becoming an Eagle Scout is a great accomplishment; being an Eagle Scout is a great responsibility. The Scout Oath and Scout Law take on new meaning; the motto and slogan take on new urgency.

The Eagle's first obligation is to live with honor. He is a marked man, a leader; for good or ill, people will follow the example he sets. He would sooner give up anything than his reputation and good name. As Shakespeare said, "Mine honor is my life; both grow in one. Take honor from me, and my life is done." The white of the Eagle badge represents honor.

The second obligation of an Eagle Scout is to be loyal. As a follower, he promised to be loyal to those above him. Now, as a leader, he must also be loyal to those below him, treating them as he would want to be treated. And he must also be loyal to his ideals, not letting others sway him from his course. The blue of the Eagle badge represents loyalty.

The Eagle Scout's third obligation is to be courageous. Stepping into his new role as a leader, he will face many challenges and obstacles. A ship in the harbor is safe, but that's not what ships are for. The Eagle must have the courage to do what is right, no matter what other people do or say. The red of the Eagle badge represents courage.

The fourth obligation of an Eagle Scout is to serve others, for a leader is above all a servant. The practice of the daily good turn leads the Eagle to a lifetime of service. He knows that only in giving of himself does he give anything of value. Just as it always has, the scroll on his badge represents service.

The final obligation of an Eagle Scout is to have vision. As a leader, he must now blaze his own trail. Just as a bald eagle soaring high above the ground can look far into the distance, so too the Eagle Scout must look far into the future. Many people will follow him; only with vision will he lead them in the right direction. The silver eagle hanging from his badge reminds the Eagle Scout of vision.

These then are the obligations of the Eagle Scout: honor, loyalty, courage, service, and vision. With these qualities, he can lead his troop, his community, and his nation toward a better tomorrow.

4. The Trail to Eagle

This segment chronicles the Scout's climb to the Eagle rank. As the text is read, the Scout walks from the back of the room to the stage. If possible, a spotlight should follow him as he walks.

Along his path are large signs showing the rank badges. (The signs from the Boy Scout Insignia Card Set work well for this.) Ideally, your signs should be double-sided so people throughout the room can see them. The signs should be spaced so that the Life sign is at the foot of the steps and the Eagle sign is on the stage. You can either mount the signs on posts or have Scouts hold them.

   The text given here is pretty general. You should modify it to fit the honoree. If he took nine months to get to First Class, don't say he took a year. If he sped through Star, don't say he stopped to rest. If he's a Venturer, talk about his crew experience.

   You can also use the text found in Troop Program Resources or the "Voice of the Eagle" text on page 60.

   We are gathered here tonight to mark the end of a long journey, a journey up the trail to Eagle.

   _____ years ago, _____ joined our troop. *(The honoree stands at the end of the aisle leading to the stage.)*

   As a new Scout, his first task was to learn about Scouting's ideals: the Oath and Law, the motto and slogan. By pledging to live by those guidelines, he became a full-fledged Scout and earned the Scout badge. *(The honoree walks forward to the Scout sign.)*

   His new badge didn't stay on his uniform long, however. He quickly worked through the Tenderfoot® requirements, memorizing the Oath and Law, going on his first campout, and learning basic first-aid skills. He was now a Tenderfoot Scout. *(The honoree walks forward to the Tenderfoot sign.)*

   As he continued to be active in the troop, he learned about nature and orienteering and knot-tying. He participated in a service project and in a program on the dangers of alcohol, drugs, and tobacco. Doing these things and more earned him the Second Class® badge. *(The honoree walks forward to the Second Class sign.)*

   Soon, a year had passed. He had been on 10 campouts and many hikes. He had mastered all the basic skills of Scouting. On _____, he became a First Class® Scout. And he truly was first class. *(The honoree walks forward to the First Class sign.)*

   At this point, he paused for a well-deserved rest. The path ahead was less clear than the path he had been following. Now he had to make some choices: which merit badges to earn, what troop office to hold, where to spend his service hours. With hard work and persistence, though, he made the decisions, completed the requirements, and earned the Star® rank. *(The honoree walks forward to the Star sign.)*

The next rank, Life®, seemed no harder than Star. But he had already done most of the easy merit badges; now he had to earn badges like: *(list a couple of the Scout's Life merit badges)*. He worked hard as a troop leader, completed more service hours, and became a Life Scout – one step away from Eagle. *(The honoree walks forward to the Life sign.)*

The going got pretty tough now. He could no longer put off those really hard badges. And now he not only had to participate in a service project, but he had to plan and lead such a project. *(Briefly describe the Scout's Eagle service project.)*

Now, finally, his Eagle project done, his merit badges earned, he stands poised at the pinnacle of Scouting. *(The honoree steps up onto the stage and stands beside the Eagle sign.)*

5. Voice of the Eagle

An unseen narrator – the Voice of the Eagle – describes the honoree's Scouting history. As he speaks, the audience watches a slideshow of pictures of the honoree as he's grown in the Scouting program. The text presented here is new; you can find the more traditional version in Troop Program Resources.

As with "Trail to Eagle," it's important that you customize the Voice of the Eagle text to fit your honoree.

This is the Voice of the Eagle, the Eagle who has watched for years as you've struggled to ascend to our aerie.

Think back for a moment, back to the day when you first joined Troop _____. How small you felt in your crisp new uniform, struggling to recite the Scout Oath and Scout Law with the other Scouts. I watched as you stole a glance upward, looking toward the clouds and wondering if you could ever achieve the summit of Scouting.

Soon, you began to advance, mastering the Oath and the Law and beginning to learn the ways of the Scout. You camped overnight and then for a weekend – and then spent an entire week away from home at summer camp. I watched you grow that week in skills and in spirit, and I saw the pride on your face as the Scoutmaster handed you your Tenderfoot badge.

It wasn't long before a year had passed. Your Tenderfoot badge was long gone, replaced by the Second Class badge and then by the badge of the First Class Scout. You had begun in earnest the climb toward Eagle, and as I watched, I could sense your determination.

But I also knew that many Scouts start off determined, only to become discouraged. For the climb from First Class to Eagle becomes harder with each step, and only a handful of Scouts reach the top. In fact, as you climbed, you could see that there were far fewer Scouts ahead of you, clearing the path, than there behind you, following in your footsteps.

Along the way, I watched you grow in other ways in Scouting. *(Briefly describe the honoree's camp staff experience, Order of the Arrow membership, or participation in a national jamboree or other high-adventure activity.)*

Then, finally, on _____, you broke through the clouds and became a Life Scout. Now, I could see clearly into your face and your heart, and I knew that someday you would join our Eagle brotherhood.

Over these past months, I've watched as you've earned the last of your merit badges, so that now ___ badges parade across your sash. I've watched you serve our troop as *(leadership position)*, reaching down constantly to help your fellow Scouts in their climb toward the summit. And I've watched you give back to your community through your Eagle Scout service project. *(Briefly describe the Scout's Eagle service project.)*

Now, I stand ready – with all the Eagles who have gone before you – to welcome you to our aerie as you join the brotherhood of Eagle Scouts.

6. The Stages of Scouting

This ceremony, adapted from the 1962 book Troop Activities, *emphasizes the progression from being a brand-new Boy Scout to becoming an Eagle Scout. This ceremony requires a new Boy Scout, a Tenderfoot Scout, a Second Class Scout, a First Class Scout, a Star Scout, and a Life Scout. These boys should be seated, in order, in the first row of the audience; the new Scout should be on the audience's left.*

Each Scout in order stands, holds his poster toward the audience, and repeats his lines. When he's through, he remains standing. Finally, the leader says his lines, and the boys sit down.

New Scout: I am a new Boy Scout. I wear the fleur-de-lis, the symbol of Scouting around the world. The three parts of the fleur-de-lis represent the three parts of the Scout Oath, which I am beginning to learn and live.

Tenderfoot Scout: I am a Tenderfoot Scout. To the fleur-de-lis on my badge have been added an eagle and shield, representing my country, and two stars, representing truth and knowledge.

Second Class Scout: I am a Second Class Scout. My badge is a scroll inscribed with the Scout motto, "Be Prepared." Suspended from this scroll is a knot, reminding me to do a good turn every day.

First Class Scout: I am a First Class Scout. My badge shows the complete Scout emblem – fleur-de-lis, eagle and shield, stars, and scroll – indicating that I have completed my basic Scout training.

Star Scout: I am a Star Scout. Before me lie unlimited opportunities, just like the stars in the night sky. I can shine as brightly as any of them.

Life Scout: I am a Life Scout, almost an Eagle. The heart on my badge shows that I've taken Scouting's lessons to heart. I am ready to spread my wings and fly.

Leader: In just a few short years, a Scout undergoes a miraculous transformation – from someone who struggles to memorize the Oath and Law to someone who lives those words, from someone who wants to go camping to someone who's been camping many times, from someone who needs to be led to someone who can lead others.

But a more miraculous transformation is yet to come, as a boy becomes an Eagle Scout.

7. The Eagle in History

A version of this piece has been floating around for many years. I never liked it much because it wasn't entirely accurate and because it didn't directly relate to the Eagle Scout. The version below attempts to correct those problems.

The use of the eagle to represent Scouting's best is very appropriate. The eagle is, of course, our national bird, adorning our coins, several state flags, and the Great Seal of the United States of America.

But the symbolism of the eagle goes back much farther in time. In fact, the eagle has symbolized humankind's best since the dawn of recorded history.

The eagle has long been a symbol of good triumphing over evil. The ancient Greeks depicted the eagle holding a serpent in its claws, much as the American eagle holds arrows and an olive branch. So too the Eagle Scout battles evil in the world with the good in himself.

Armies from ancient Rome to nineteenth-century Europe have marched under eagle standards. Sioux warriors adorned their war bonnets with eagle feathers. Since 1912, an army of Eagle Scouts, more than two million strong, has gone out to build a better world for themselves and their fellow men.

Many cultures, watching the eagle fly toward the sun, have associated the bird with their sun gods. To the Assyrians, for example, the eagle represented the sun god Ashur; and in early Christianity, the eagle symbolized the ascension of Christ into heaven. Today the Eagle Scout continues to fly high, his gaze always fixed on his goals.

For countless centuries, the eagle has represented victory and valor, grace and beauty. The Eagle Scout represents those things, as well as the values embodied in the Scout Oath and Law.

The eagle is a rare creature. When you see one flying, you can't help but stop and watch its graceful, exuberant soaring. The Eagle Scout is a rare creature, too. Just watch him fly.

8. An Eagle Poem

You can use the text here to introduce one of the poems printed in Appendix B. Or, if you have an amateur poet in your troop, consider asking him or her to compose a poem for the occasion. After the poem is read, you might want to present a framed copy to the honoree – anyone with a computer and laser printer can create a presentation-quality copy of the poem.

Since whichever poem you choose is likely to be rather short, you may want to use this Eagle segment in conjunction with one of the others from this chapter.

Master of Ceremonies: Before we move on to the presentation of the Eagle badge, it's appropriate that we pause to reflect on the

badge's meaning. To give us a sense of that meaning, I'd like to ask
_____ to present a special poem at this time.

Reader: *(Reads one of the poems from Appendix B.)*

9. Unscripted Eagle Segments

In Chapter 3, I mentioned the idea of having people who know the honoree well share a few anecdotes about his Scouting journey. This can work well after "Trail to Eagle" because it adds some color to that potential monochrome presentation. The key is to select two or three people (Scouts or older adults) who can talk about different phases of the honoree's life. Ideally, each person will script his remarks and focus on telling a couple of colorful anecdotes. A limit of perhaps 300 words per person seems appropriate.

Here's another idea, one that would work especially well with an Order of the Arrow–themed ceremony: Put a jar of different colored pony beads on the lectern and ask anybody who feels so inspired to come up, pick out a bead, and tell the audience why the bead's color reminds him or her of the honoree. (For example, the neighbor medic might choose red because it reminds him of the countless times the honoree came over to get bandaged up.) After telling their brief *stories, the speakers then add their beads to a coup feather, which is simply an imitation eagle feather attached to a leather string, perhaps dangling from a hiking staff. (Be sure to have someone write down what all the colors stand for and who picked them, so the honoree can have a permanent record.) If you try this idea, people some advance notice before asking them to come forward; otherwise, there may be an awkward pause while everyone tries to think of stories. Also, keep the program moving and cut off the reminiscences when the program starts to drag.*

One more unscripted Eagle segment that can work, especially when you have multiple honorees, is to do a question-and-answer session, much like on a late-night talk show. Seat the master of ceremonies and honoree in a comfortable setting and have the master of ceremonies ask the honoree about his Eagle project, his most memorable or embarrassing Scouting moment, his college plans (if he's a senior), etc. With honorees who can think on their feet, this can be a lot of fun. The "Late Night" script on page 118 uses this Eagle segment.

Chapter 6

The Presentation of the Eagle Badge

The centerpiece of the Eagle Scout court of honor

The Presentation of the Eagle Badge

*It is a fine moment in his life and the lives of those near
and dear to him when he receives the cherished badge –
the recognition of his achievements.*
—The Boy Scout Encyclopedia, *1962*

Everything that has happened up until now has been in preparation for the actual badge presentation. By now, the honoree and the audience are ready to move right to the big moment.

Unlike the other parts of the court of honor, where you have a lot of choices to make, the presentation phase is pretty standard and straightforward. About the only things that might change are who will actually be participating and whether the honoree is already on stage. (You can download this text from **www.eaglebook.com/scripts/**.)

A word about families is important here. Gone are the days when most Scouts lived at home with both of their biological parents. Today's Scouts often live with a single parent, stepparents, adoptive parents, legal guardians, or grandparents.

As you're planning the presentation phase, then, you'll need to take into account which family members will be participating. Don't worry, for example, if there's no father present to receive an Eagle lapel pin – or if you need a lapel pin for both the birth father and the stepfather. Just adjust the script accordingly.

In planning the presentation sequence, try to picture it in your mind. Where is the Scout going to stand? What about his parents? What is the Scout going to do with all the certificates, plaques, belt buckles, and so forth that are handed to him? (Hint: Have a place for him to set them down.) Is he going to have a hand free to shake with his Scoutmaster?

Finally, what are he and his parents going to do during the next part of the ceremony, the closing period? Answering all these questions beforehand can help you avoid some awkward moments during the ceremony.

Introduction of Scout

Master of Ceremonies: It's now time for the highlight of our program: the presentation of the Eagle Scout Award. I'd like to ask Scoutmaster _____ to come forward to make the appropriate presentations.

Scoutmaster: Will the honor guard please escort the candidate forward. *(The honor guard consists of two or three Scouts, either Eagles, soon-to-be Eagles, or members of the honoree's patrol.)*

(At this point, you have two choices: the Scoutmaster can recount the honoree's Scouting history – assuming you haven't covered that in the Eagle segment – or the Scout himself can talk about what Scouting has meant to him. If the Scout is a good speaker, I strongly recommend the second choice.)

Scout's History (by Scoutmaster)

Scoutmaster: We have heard a lot tonight about what it takes to be an Eagle Scout. At this time, I'd like to tell you a little bit about our honoree's Scouting experiences. *(Presents a brief summary of the honoree's Scouting history. This shouldn't be a dry summary of badges earned and offices held. Instead, tell some interesting things the boy has done, focusing on his growth in Scouting: "When a pint-sized Johnny Jones showed up in a brand-new quart-sized uniform to join our troop five years ago, I had no idea he'd grow up to be a gallon-sized Eagle Scout with a ten-gallon heart." Give special emphasis to the Eagle Scout service project.)*

Scout's Personal Statement

Scoutmaster: We have heard a lot tonight about what it means to be an Eagle Scout. Now our honoree will have the chance to tell us a little about what the Eagle badge and Scouting mean to him.

Honoree: *(Talks about what he's learned in the program, what the highlights of his time in Scouting have been, and what being an Eagle means to him. If he has no idea what to say, suggest that he answer two questions: "What has the Scouting experience meant to me?" and "What am I going to do about it?" Done right, this can be a very moving presentation. You should work with him in developing his comments; make sure he uses notes or a script. If the Scout wants to give the Scoutmaster or a mentor a gift, this would be an appropriate time. However, his statement shouldn't be simply a list of thank-yous like an awards-show acceptance speech.)*

The Charge

The Eagle charge bridges the gap between what the boy has done as a Scout and what he is now expected to do as a leader. The charge should be given by someone important in the boy's life, preferably an adult Eagle Scout.

Scoutmaster: Becoming an Eagle Scout is not the end of a journey; it is merely the beginning. As an Eagle, you have far greater responsibilities than you had before. To explain those responsibilities, I'd like _____ to come forward and give the Eagle charge.

"Charger": *(Presents one of the Eagle charges from Appendix A or uses his or her own text.)*

Eagle Promise

Scoutmaster: As our court of honor began tonight, you joined with your fellow Scouts in repeating the Scout Oath. Now, you will stand alone and repeat a new oath, the Eagle Scout Promise. Though the words you say are similar to those you've said so many times before, tonight they will mean more to you than they ever have. When you pledge yourself on your sacred honor, you will be sealing your oath with the words that closed the Declaration of Independence.

I'd like all Eagle Scouts in the audience to stand at this time and rededicate themselves by repeating the Eagle Scout Promise with our new Eagle Scout.

Please make the Scout sign and repeat after me:

> I reaffirm my allegiance
> To the three promises of the Scout Oath.
> I thoughtfully recognize
> And take upon myself
> The obligations and responsibilities
> Of an Eagle Scout.
> On my honor I will do my best
> To make my training and example,
> My rank and my influence
> Count strongly for better Scouting
> And for better citizenship
> In my troop,
> In my community,
> And in my contacts with other people.
> To this I pledge my sacred honor.

Two. *(To Eagles in audience)* Please be seated.

The Presentation

Note: if the honoree doesn't live in a typical nuclear family, adjust this section as appropriate. For suggestions, see page 66 and the sidebar on page 29. This is also a great place to involve siblings, especially an older brother who's an Eagle Scout or a younger brother who's a Tiger Cub.

Scoutmaster: Would the honor guard please escort the candidate's parents forward.

(Addressing the honoree) _____, your parents have undoubtedly been your primary source of help and strength.

No one will ever know the unnumbered acts of self-sacrifice from your mother. I'd like your mother to pin the Eagle medal on your uniform. *(She does so.)*

In recognition of your mother's devotion, please present her with this Eagle mother's pin. *(Scout pins on mother's pin.)*

Your father has been the source of much advice and guidance along the Eagle trail, so I'd like him to present the Eagle Scout certificate to you. *(He does so.)*

In return, please present your father with this Eagle lapel pin. *(He does so.)*

(Facing the audience) And now, it gives me great pleasure to present to you our newest Eagle Scout, _____!

(The audience responds with a standing ovation, which you may need to initiate.)

Other Presentations

Scoutmaster: We're not through yet, however.

(At this time, any other presentations – from the troop, chartered organization, etc. – are made. The Scoutmaster may also read excerpts from congratulatory letters received; see page 149 for more information. When he is finished, he congratulates the honoree and sits down. The master of ceremonies then moves to the closing period, as discussed on page 30.)

Chapter 7

Complete Ceremonies

Eight complete, ready-to-use scripts, each with its own theme

Complete Ceremonies

Here are several Eagle Scout recognition ceremonies that have been used successfully in different types of councils. These ceremonies are dignified and inspirational. If well conducted they should be impressive.
—Troop Ceremonies, *1955*

Throughout this book, I've talked about the various components of the court-of-honor ceremony. This chapter puts those parts together in eight ready-to-use ceremonies, which you can download from **www.eaglebook .com/scripts/**.

As you'll see, each of these ceremonies has its own theme, which is referred to throughout the script. Despite their variety, however, they are all built on the framework that I described in Chapter 3.

1. Eagle Mountain

The journey to Eagle is sometimes compared to a climb up a mountain, and the central feature of this ceremony is a reading that dramatizes that climb. An excellent way to present this reading is to couple it with a slideshow of mountain images interspersed with pictures of the honoree showing his growth in Scouting.

Opening Period

Master of Ceremonies: Good evening. My name is _____, and I'm pleased to serve as master of ceremonies as we honor Scout _____ for his ascent up the Eagle Mountain. This is indeed a special night in the life of this Scout and this troop.

Before we begin our program, I'd like to introduce a few special people. *(Introduces key troop leaders, representatives of the chartered organization, presenters, and special guests.)*

I'd like to remind you all that there will be a reception honoring our new Eagle immediately following the ceremony. *(Other announcements, as necessary, are made here.)*

Now please rise for the invocation, presented by _____, and remain standing for the presentation of the colors and the Pledge of Allegiance.

Religious Leader or Chaplain Aide: *(Presents an invocation.)*

Scouts: *(Present the colors. One Scout leads the group in the Pledge of Allegiance.)*

Master of Ceremonies: I now call on _____, as a representative of the Boy Scouts of America, to officially convene this court of honor.

BSA Representative: By the power vested in me by the National Council of the Boy Scouts of America, I declare this court of honor to be duly convened for the sole purpose of presenting the Eagle Scout Award to _____.

Scouting Segment: Scout Law Candle Ceremony

(On a table at the front is a candelabrum with 12 candles, representing the points of the Scout Law, along with a 13th candle, representing the Spirit of Scouting. A Scout stands behind each of the Scout Law candles. Each Scout's part is printed on a card and laid on the table in front of him.)

Leader *(holding lighted "Spirit" candle)*: This candle represents the Spirit of Scouting, a spirit which burns brightly in the heart of every Scout. Let us renew our spirit by reminding ourselves of the meaning of the Scout Law.

(He hands the candle to the first Scout. As this Scout reads his part, he lights the candle in front of him. When he has finished, he hands the candle to the next Scout. Continue in this manner until all 12 Scouts have finished.)

First Scout: A Scout is trustworthy. A Scout's honor is to be trusted. If he were to violate his honor by telling a lie, or by cheating, or by not doing exactly a given task, when trusted on his honor, he may be directed to hand over his Scout badge.

Second Scout: A Scout is loyal. He is loyal to all to whom loyalty is due: his Scout leader, his home, and parents and country.

Third Scout: A Scout is helpful. He must be prepared at any time to save life, help injured persons, and share the home duties. He must do at least one good turn to somebody every day.

Fourth Scout: A Scout is friendly. He is a friend to all and a brother to every other Scout.

Fifth Scout: A Scout is courteous. He is polite to all, especially to women, children, old people, and the weak and helpless. He must not take pay for being helpful or courteous.

Sixth Scout: A Scout is kind. He is a friend to animals. He will not kill nor hurt any living creature needlessly, but will strive to save and protect all harmless life.

Seventh Scout: A Scout is obedient. He obeys his parents, Scoutmaster, patrol leader, and all other duly constituted authorities.

Eighth Scout: A Scout is cheerful. He smiles whenever he can. His obedience to orders is prompt and cheery. He never shirks nor grumbles at hardships.

Ninth Scout: A Scout is thrifty. He does not wantonly destroy property. He works faithfully, wastes nothing, and makes the best use of his opportunities. He saves his money so that he may pay his own way, be generous to those in need, and helpful to worthy objects. He may work for pay, but must not receive tips for courtesies or good turns.

Tenth Scout: A Scout is brave. He has the courage to face danger in spite of fear, and to stand up for the right against the coaxing of friends or the jeers or threats of enemies, and defeat does not down him.

Eleventh Scout: A Scout is clean. He keeps clean in body and thought, stands for clean speech, clean sport, clean habits, and travels with a clean crowd.

Twelfth Scout: A Scout is reverent. He is reverent toward God. He is faithful in his religious duties, and respects the convictions of others in matters of custom and religion.

(The last Scout blows out the "Spirit" candle. The Scouts then return to their seats.)

Eagle Segment: The Legend of Eagle Mountain

(The following text is read by an unseen narrator as slides of the honoree and of mountain scenes are projected on a screen at the front of the room.)

Narrator: Early one morning a young boy stood at a trailhead. Before him rose a mighty mountain, which seemed all the mightier when compared with his smallness.

A trail led to the mountain and then up it to incredible heights before vanishing in the clouds. On this trail the boy could see other boys and young men, some of whom turned and beckoned him to follow.

The boy began to climb, refusing perhaps to believe that he could ever reach the top. At first the trail rose gently, and the boy had many companions. But soon he began to sweat and breathe heavily, and many of his companions turned away. And still the boy climbed.

At times he climbed quickly. At times he climbed slowly. At times he had to go down a little way to find another path or stop a while to catch his breath. But still he climbed. The trail became steeper, the air thinner, but the climber scarcely noticed for he had, along the way, become stronger of body and hardier of spirit. And still he climbed.

And finally in the cool peace of eveningtime, he stood alone at the top of the world and looked around him. To the left he saw a fiery golden sunset. To the right he saw a diamond-studded, silky-black night sky. Behind him he saw the trail that he had followed and the hikers who were following in his footsteps.

And in front of him he saw another mountain. And another. And another. And a whole procession of mountains marching off to the horizon. But the young man (for now he *was* a man) knew that none of these other mountains was insurmountable, that all could and would be climbed. For he had learned many skills in the climbing of the first mountain, and he would carry those skills with him long after this mountain was forgotten.

And besides, he could begin climbing the next mountain tomorrow. Tonight he would rest and celebrate and ponder the journey that he had completed. And so tonight, we pause to rest and celebrate and honor this fine young man, Eagle Scout _____, as he stands at the top of the world and looks around him.

The Presentation of the Eagle Badge

Master of Ceremonies: It's now time for the highlight of our program: the presentation of the Eagle Scout Award. I'd like to ask Scoutmaster _____ to come forward to make the appropriate presentations.

Scoutmaster: Will the honor guard please escort the candidate forward. *(The honor guard consists of two or three Scouts, either Eagles, soon-to-be Eagles, or members of the honoree's patrol.)*

Scoutmaster: We have heard a lot tonight about what it means to be an Eagle Scout. Now our honoree will have the chance to tell us a little about what his climb up the Eagle Mountain has meant to him.

Honoree: *(Talks about what he's learned in the program, what the highlights of his time in Scouting have been, and what being an Eagle means to him. If the Scout wants to give the Scoutmaster or a mentor a gift, this would be an appropriate time.)*

Scoutmaster: Becoming an Eagle Scout is not the end of a journey; it is merely the beginning. So where do you go from here? _____ is here to tell you.

"Charger": Congratulations! You've made it. You've climbed the Eagle Mountain. I applaud your achievement.

But now it's time to look toward the future, toward those others mountains out on the horizon.

How are you going to climb them? The same way you climbed the Eagle Mountain. Just remember the things you learned on your way to Eagle, and you'll be able to climb any mountain, to overcome any obstacle.

Do you remember when you first looked up at the Eagle Mountain? How high it seemed back then. But you took that first step along the trail and began climbing. One step at a time, you followed the trail blazed by others. Then, when that path faded away, you blazed your own trail, a trail that others are now following.

And finally, always keeping your eye on the goal, you reached the top.

You have many mountains waiting to be climbed. Some may seem insurmountable, but they can all be conquered. Just set your goal, take that first step, follow the blazed trail until it's time to blaze your own, and always keep your eye on the goal.

May God be with you as you begin your next climb!

Scoutmaster: Many times over the last few years, you've joined with your fellow Scouts in repeating the Scout Oath. Now, you will stand alone and repeat a new oath, the Eagle Scout Promise. Though the words you say are similar to those you've said so many times before, tonight they will mean more to you than they ever have. When you pledge yourself on your sacred honor, you will be sealing your oath with the words that closed the Declaration of Independence.

I'd like all Eagle Scouts in the audience to stand at this time and rededicate themselves by repeating the Eagle Scout Promise with our new Eagle Scout.

Please make the Scout sign and repeat after me:

> I reaffirm my allegiance
> To the three promises of the Scout Oath.
> I thoughtfully recognize
> And take upon myself
> The obligations and responsibilities
> Of an Eagle Scout.
> On my honor I will do my best
> To make my training and example,
> My rank and my influence
> Count strongly for better Scouting
> And for better citizenship
> In my troop,
> In my community,
> And in my contacts with other people.
> To this I pledge my sacred honor.

Two. *(To Eagles in audience)* Please be seated.

Scoutmaster: Would the honor guard please escort the candidate's parents forward.

(Addressing the honoree) _____, your parents have undoubtedly been your primary source of help and strength.

No one will ever know the unnumbered acts of self-sacrifice from your mother. I'd like your mother to pin the Eagle medal on your uniform. *(She does so.)*

In recognition of your mother's devotion, please present her with this Eagle mother's pin. *(Scout pins on mother's pin.)*

Your father has been the source of much advice and guidance along the Eagle trail, so I'd like him to present the Eagle Scout certificate to you. *(He does so.)*

In return, please present your father with this Eagle lapel pin. *(He does so.)*

(Facing the audience) And now, it gives me great pleasure to present to you our newest Eagle Scout, _____!

(The audience responds with a standing ovation, which you may need to initiate.)

Scoutmaster: We're not through yet, however.

(At this time, any other presentations – from the troop, chartered organization, etc. – are made. The Scoutmaster may also read excerpts from congratulatory letters received. When he is finished, he congratulates the honoree and sits down.)

Closing Period

Master of Ceremonies: Tonight has indeed been a special night. Thank you all for coming out and participating in this wonderful event. Let's give our new Eagle Scout one more round of applause.

I now call on _____ to give our benediction.

Religious Leader or Chaplain Aide: *(Gives benediction.)*

Master of Ceremonies: Again, thank you for coming. Please join us at the reception. Good night.

2. The Ranks of Scouting

If this is your troop's first Eagle court of honor, or if most of the audience members are unfamiliar with the advancement program, consider using this ceremony. In dramatic fashion, it describes each of the ranks of Scouting and outlines in detail the skills the Eagle Scout has mastered.

Opening Period

Master of Ceremonies: Good evening. My name is _____, and I'm pleased to serve as master of ceremonies as we honor Scout _____ for attaining Scouting's highest rank, the Eagle Scout Award. This is a great moment worthy of celebration.

Before we begin our program, I'd like to introduce a few special people. *(Introduces key troop leaders, representatives of the chartered organization, presenters, and special guests.)*

I'd like to remind you all that there will be a reception honoring our new Eagle immediately following the ceremony. *(Other announcements, as necessary, are made here.)*

Now please rise for the invocation, presented by _____, and remain standing for the presentation of the colors.

Religious Leader or Chaplain Aide: *(Presents an invocation.)*

Scouts: *(Present the colors. One Scout leads the group in the Pledge of Allegiance and the Scout Oath.)*

Master of Ceremonies: I now call on _____, as a representative of the Boy Scouts of America, to officially convene this court of honor.

BSA Representative: By the power vested in me by the National Council of the Boy Scouts of America, I declare this court of honor to be duly convened for the sole purpose of presenting the Eagle Scout Award to _____.

Scouting Segment: The Stages of Scouting

(This ceremony requires a new Boy Scout, a Tenderfoot Scout, a Second Class Scout, a First Class Scout, a Star Scout, and a Life Scout. These boys should be seated, in order, in the first row of the audience; the new Scout should be on the audience's left. Each Scout in order stands, holds his poster toward the audience, and repeats his lines. When he's through, he remains standing. Finally, the master of ceremonies says his lines, and the boys sit down.)

Master of Ceremonies: We are indeed here to honor Eagle Scout _____. But this is not the first time he's been recognized before a court of honor. Six times before he has stood here: first when he received his Scout badge, then when he earned each rank leading up to Eagle. And each time he has seemed a little taller, a little stronger, a little more dedicated to the ideals of Scouting.

Let's take a moment to reflect back on the steps he took on the way to Eagle.

New Scout: I am a new Boy Scout. I wear the fleur-de-lis, the symbol of Scouting around the world. The three parts of the fleur-de-lis represent the three parts of the Scout Oath, which I am beginning to learn and live.

Tenderfoot Scout: I am a Tenderfoot Scout. To the fleur-de-lis on my badge have been added an eagle and shield, representing my country, and two stars, representing truth and knowledge.

Second Class Scout: I am a Second Class Scout. My badge is a scroll inscribed with the Scout motto, "Be Prepared." Suspended from this scroll is a knot, reminding me to do a good turn every day.

First Class Scout: I am a First Class Scout. My badge shows the complete Scout emblem – fleur-de-lis, eagle and shield, stars, and scroll – indicating that I have completed my basic Scout training.

Star Scout: I am a Star Scout. Before me lie unlimited opportunities, just like the stars in the night sky. I can shine as brightly as any of them.

Life Scout: I am a Life Scout, almost an Eagle. The heart on my badge shows that I've taken Scouting's lessons to heart. I am ready to spread my wings and fly.

Leader: Yes, in just a few short years, _____ has undergone a miraculous transformation – from someone who struggled to memorize the Oath and Law to someone who lives those words, from someone who wanted to go camping to someone who's been camping many times, from someone who needed to be led to someone who can lead others.

Eagle Segment: The Requirements of an Eagle Scout

Leader: But what exactly does it mean to be an Eagle? We've asked Scouter _____ to tell us.

Scouter _____: We are here tonight to honor a young man as he becomes an Eagle Scout. As we do so, it's important to reflect on what it means to be an Eagle Scout.

The 1938 *Handbook for Scoutmasters* put it this way:

> The badges which accompany his advancement and which the Scout wears on his Uniform are not to show that he has "passed certain tests." There should be no past tense implied! On the contrary, each badge cries out "I can, right now and here!"

So what can the Eagle Scout do? Let's take a look at some of the things he has done in preparing to be an Eagle Scout.

In terms of badges, he has earned the Scout badge and the ranks of Tenderfoot, Second Class, First Class, Star, Life, and finally Eagle. Along the way, he earned 12 required merit badges and nine elective merit badges, served in troop leadership positions for a total of 16 months, and spent at least 13 hours on service projects, not including the many hours he spent on his Eagle Scout service project. In all, he has completed approximately 325 different requirements.

So what have these requirements taught him? Who *is* the Eagle Scout?

First and foremost, of course, he is an outdoorsman. He knows how to camp, swim, hike, use woods tools, build a fire, use a camp stove, and find his way with map and compass. He's spent at least 20 days and nights camping out in a tent he pitched on a site he selected. Many of those times he planned his own menu and cooked his own food.

The Eagle Scout is comfortable with nature. He can identify local animals and plants, including poisonous plants. He understands the causes of water, land, and air pollution and developed a project to solve an environmental problem.

He embodies the Scout motto, "Be Prepared." He knows how to treat fractures, head injuries, hypothermia, convulsions, frostbite, burns, abdominal pain, muscle cramps, even knocked-out teeth. He knows what to do in case of fire, explosion, desert emergency, motor-vehicle accident, mountain accident, food poisoning, gas leak, earthquake, flood, tornado, hurricane, atomic emergency, and avalanche.

The Eagle Scout is a good citizen. He's been to a city meeting and knows how the city government is organized. He knows who his U.S. Senators and Representative are and has written a letter to one of them about a national issue. He's read the Declaration of Independence and the U.S. Constitution.

He knows how to manage his money and understands the risks and benefits of putting his money in savings bonds, mutual funds, common stock, and real estate. He has set financial goals and worked toward achieving those goals.

The Eagle Scout has also set and worked toward fitness goals. He's competed against himself in tests of aerobic endurance, flexibility, and muscular strength. He knows what it means to be physically, mentally, and socially fit.

He's a good family member. He knows what things are important to the members of his family and has talked to his family about finances, drug abuse, and growing up.

All of these things he did in order to earn the merit badges required for Eagle. Beyond those, he earned nine elective merit badges, which introduced him to such subjects as: *(list some of the honoree's elective merit badges here)*

So what is an Eagle Scout? Well, to quote that old *Handbook for Scoutmasters* again, he is a young man "who is qualified to help others as well as take care of himself." His badge is not "a decoration, but rather a symbol of knowledge and ability."

The Presentation of the Eagle Badge

Master of Ceremonies: It's now time for the highlight of our program: the presentation of the Eagle Scout Award. I'd like to ask Scoutmaster _____ to come forward to make the appropriate presentations.

Scoutmaster: Will the honor guard please escort the candidate forward. *(The honor guard consists of two or three Scouts, either Eagles, soon-to-be Eagles, or members of the honoree's patrol.)*

Scoutmaster: We have heard a lot tonight about what it takes to be an Eagle Scout. Now I'd like to tell you a little bit about our honoree's Scouting experiences. *(Presents a brief summary of the honoree's Scouting history. This shouldn't be a dry summary of badges earned and offices* *held. Instead, tell some interesting things the boy has done, focusing on his growth in Scouting.)*

Scoutmaster: By becoming an Eagle Scout you gain more than a pretty medal to wear. You also gain some important responsibilities. I'd like to ask _____ to outline some of those responsibilities for you.

"Charger": Becoming an Eagle Scout is a great accomplishment; being an Eagle Scout is a great responsibility. As an Eagle, the Scout Oath and Scout Law should take on new meaning for you; the motto and slogan take on new urgency.

As an Eagle, your first obligation is to live with honor. You are a marked man, a leader; for good or ill, people will follow the example you set. Give up anything before you give up your reputation and good name. As Shakespeare said, "Mine honor is my life; both grow in one. Take honor from me, and my life is done." Let the white of the Eagle badge remind you of honor.

Your second obligation as an Eagle Scout is to be loyal. As a follower, you promised to be loyal to those above you. Now, as a leader, you must also be loyal to those below you, treating them as you would want to be treated. And you must also be loyal to your ideals, not letting others sway you from your course. Let the blue of the Eagle badge remind you of loyalty.

Your third obligation as an Eagle Scout is to be courageous. Stepping into your new role as a leader, you will face many challenges and obstacles. A ship in the harbor is safe, but that's not what ships are for. You must have the courage to do what is right, whatever other people do or say. Let the red of the Eagle badge remind you of courage.

Your fourth obligation is to serve others, for a leader is above all a servant. Let the practice of the daily good turn become a lifetime of service, for only in giving of yourself do you give anything of value. Just as it always has, let the scroll on your badge remind you of service.

Your final obligation as an Eagle Scout is to have vision. As a leader, you must now blaze your own trail. Just as a bald eagle soaring high above the ground can look far into the distance, so too must you look far into the future. Many people will follow you; only with vision will you lead them in the right direction. Let the silver eagle hanging from your badge reminds you of vision.

These then are your obligations as an Eagle Scout: honor, loyalty, courage, service, and vision. By meeting those obligations, you can lead your troop, your community, your nation toward a better tomorrow.

Scoutmaster: When we began our program tonight, you joined with your fellow Scouts in repeating the Scout Oath. Now, you will stand alone and repeat a new oath, the Eagle Scout Promise. Though the words you say are similar to those you've said so many times before, tonight they will mean more to you than they ever have. When you pledge yourself on your sacred honor, you will be sealing your oath with the words that closed the Declaration of Independence.

I'd like all Eagle Scouts in the audience to stand at this time and rededicate themselves by repeating the Eagle Scout Promise with our new Eagle Scout.

Please make the Scout sign and repeat after me:

> I reaffirm my allegiance
> To the three promises of the Scout Oath.
> I thoughtfully recognize
> And take upon myself
> The obligations and responsibilities
> Of an Eagle Scout.
> On my honor I will do my best
> To make my training and example,
> My rank and my influence
> Count strongly for better Scouting
> And for better citizenship
> In my troop,

In my community,
And in my contacts with other people.
To this I pledge my sacred honor.

Two. *(To Eagles in audience)* Please be seated.

Scoutmaster: Would the honor guard please escort the candidate's parents forward.

(Addressing the honoree) _____, your parents have undoubtedly been your primary source of help and strength.

No one will ever know the unnumbered acts of self-sacrifice from your mother. I'd like your mother to pin the Eagle medal on your uniform. *(She does so.)*

In recognition of your mother's devotion, please present her with this Eagle mother's pin. *(Scout pins on mother's pin.)*

Your father has been the source of much advice and guidance along the Eagle trail, so I'd like him to present the Eagle Scout certificate to you. *(He does so.)*

In return, please present your father with this Eagle lapel pin. *(He does so.)*

(Facing the audience) And now, it gives me great pleasure to present to you our newest Eagle Scout, _____!

(The audience responds with a standing ovation, which you may need to initiate.)

Scoutmaster: We're not through yet, however.

(At this time, any other presentations – from the troop, chartered organization, etc. – are made. The Scoutmaster may also read excerpts from congratulatory letters received. When he is finished, he congratulates the honoree and sits down.)

Closing Period

Master of Ceremonies: Tonight has indeed been a special night. Thank you all for coming out and participating in this wonderful event. Let's give our new Eagle Scout one more round of applause.

I now call on _____ to give our benediction.

Religious Leader or Chaplain Aide: *(Gives benediction.)*

Master of Ceremonies: Again, thank you for coming. Please join us at the reception. Good night.

3. Trail to Eagle

This ceremony follows the honoree along the trail to Eagle; it's especially appropriate for a boy who was a Cub Scout. As a narrator describes his journey, the honoree walks from the back of the room to the stage. You should customize the narrative to accurately describe the honoree's Scouting career. In particular, leave out the Venturing content if the honoree is not a Venturer.

The next ceremony, "Voice of the Eagle," uses a somewhat different approach to describing the Scout's progress through the ranks. You may want to combine elements of the two ceremonies.

Opening Period

Master of Ceremonies: Good evening. My name is _____, and I'm pleased to serve as master of ceremonies as we honor Scout _____ for attaining Scouting's highest rank, the Eagle Scout Award. This is a great moment worthy of celebration.

Before we begin our program, I'd like to introduce a few special people. *(Introduces key troop leaders, representatives of the chartered organization, presenters, and special guests.)*

I'd like to remind you all that there will be a reception honoring our new Eagle immediately following the ceremony. *(Other announcements, as necessary, are made here.)*

Now please rise for the invocation, presented by _____, and remain standing for the presentation of the colors.

Religious Leader or Chaplain Aide: *(Presents an invocation.)*

Scouts: *(Present the colors. One Scout leads the group in the Pledge of Allegiance and the Scout Oath.)*

Master of Ceremonies: I now call on _____, as a representative of the Boy Scouts of America, to officially convene this court of honor.

BSA Representative: By the power vested in me by the National Council of the Boy Scouts of America, I declare this court of honor to be duly convened for the sole purpose of presenting the Eagle Scout Award to _____.

Scouting Segment: Scouting's Codes of Conduct

Master of Ceremonies: We began our program tonight with the Scout Oath, a promise that Scout _____ has recited many times. The Scout Oath is not the only promise he's made, however; just as the Scout Law is not the only set of rules he's ever followed. At this time, I'd like Scouter _____ to tell us about some of the other codes of conduct our honoree has followed during his Scouting career.

Scouter _____: The Scouting program is designed to grow with the boy. Tiger Cub activities, for example, are quite simple when compared with those of a Boy Scout troop. And we require much more of Boy Scouts than we do of Tiger Cubs.

Tiger Cubs, in case you've forgotten, are first-grade Cub Scouts. Like their older brothers, one of the first things they do is learn the Cub Scout promise:

I, *(name)*, promise to do my best
To do my duty to God and my country,
To help other people, and
To obey the Law of the Pack.

The Law reads as follows:

The Cub Scout follows Akela.
The Cub Scout helps the pack go.
The pack helps the Cub Scout grow.
The Cub Scout gives goodwill.

The motto of the Cub Scouts is "Do Your Best."

The next step, of course, is Boy Scouting, where boys learn the Oath and the Law that we say at each of our meetings. Boy Scouting also has a motto – "Be Prepared" – and a slogan – "Do a Good Turn Daily."

[Many Scouts, like our honoree, go on to participate in Venturing, Scouting's program for older youths. Venturers recite their own solemn oath:

As a Venturer, I promise to do my duty to God and
help strengthen America, to help others, and to seek
truth, fairness, and adventure in our world.

Venturers also live by a unique code:

As a Venturer, I believe that America's strength lies in our trust in God and in the courage, strength, and traditions of our people.

I will, therefore, be faithful in my religious duties and will maintain a personal sense of honor in my own life.

I will treasure my American heritage and will do all I can to preserve and enrich it.

I will recognize the dignity and worth of all humanity and will use fair play and goodwill in my daily life.

I will acquire the Venturing attitude that seeks the truth in all things and adventure on the frontiers of our changing world.]

During his Scouting career, our honoree has learned and striven to obey all these promises, oaths, laws, mottoes, and slogans. Later tonight, he will repeat one more promise, the Eagle Scout Promise. The important thing to remember – and this applies to all of us – is that we shouldn't forget the promises we've made before just because we're making a new promise now. It's still important to do our best, to help other people, to follow Akela and give goodwill, to be prepared, and to do a good turn daily.

The Scout Oath, the Scout Law, and all the rest are not just for Scouts; they're for life.

Eagle Segment: Trail to Eagle

(As the text is read, the Scout walks from the back of the room to the stage. If possible, a spotlight should follow him as he walks. Along his path are large signs showing the rank badges. The signs should be spaced so that the Life sign is at the foot of the steps and the Eagle sign is on the stage. The text given here is pretty general. You should modify it to fit the honoree.)

Narrator: We are gathered here tonight to mark the end of a long journey, a journey up the trail to Eagle.

_____ years ago, _____ joined our troop. *(The honoree stands at the end of the aisle leading to the stage.)*

As a new Scout, his first task was to learn about Scouting's ideals: the Oath and Law, the motto and slogan. By pledging to live by those guidelines, he became a full-fledged Scout and earned the Scout badge. *(The honoree walks forward to the Scout sign.)*

His new badge didn't stay on his uniform long, however. He quickly worked through the Tenderfoot requirements, memorizing the Oath and Law, going on his first campout, and learning basic first-aid skills. He was now a Tenderfoot Scout. *(The honoree walks forward to the Tenderfoot sign.)*

As he continued to be active in the troop, he learned about nature and orienteering and knot-tying. He participated in a service project and in a program on the dangers of alcohol, drugs, and tobacco. Doing these things and more earned him the Second Class Badge. *(The honoree walks forward to the Second Class sign.)*

Soon, a year had passed. He had been on 10 campouts and many hikes. He had mastered all the basic skills of Scouting. On _____, he became a First Class Scout. And he truly was first class. *(The honoree walks forward to the First Class sign.)*

At this point, he paused for a well-deserved rest. The path ahead was less clear than the path he had been following. Now he had to make some choices: which merit badges to earn, what troop office to hold, where to spend his service hours. With hard work and persistence, though, he made the decisions, completed the requirements, and earned the Star rank. *(The honoree walks forward to the Star sign.)*

The next rank seemed no harder than Star. But he had already done most of the easy merit badges; now he had to earn badges like: (list a couple of the Scout's Life merit badges). He worked hard as a troop leader, completed more service hours, and became a Life Scout – one step away from Eagle. *(The honoree walks forward to the Life sign.)*

The going got pretty tough now. He could no longer put off those really hard badges. And now he not only had to participate in a service project, but he had to plan and lead such a project. *(Briefly describe the Scout's Eagle service project.)*

Now, finally, his Eagle project done, his merit badges earned, he stands poised at the pinnacle of Scouting. *(The honoree steps up onto the stage and stands beside the Eagle sign.)*

The Presentation of the Eagle Badge

Master of Ceremonies: It's now time for the highlight of our program: the presentation of the Eagle Scout Award. I'd like to ask Scoutmaster _____ to come forward to make the appropriate presentations.

Scoutmaster: We have heard a lot tonight about what it means to be an Eagle Scout. Now our honoree will have the chance to tell us a little about what being an Eagle Scout means to him.

Honoree: *(Talks about what he's learned in the program, what the highlights of his time in Scouting have been, and what being an Eagle means to him. If the Scout wants to give the Scoutmaster or a mentor a gift, this would be an appropriate time.)*

Scoutmaster: Becoming an Eagle Scout is a great honor; it's also a great responsibility. At this time, I'd like to ask _____ to remind you of what is required of you as an Eagle Scout.

"Charger": During your time in Scouting, you have learned and lived the Cub Scout Promise, the Law of the Pack, the Cub Scout motto, [the Venturing Oath and Code,] and of course the Scout Oath, Law, motto, and slogan.

Each time you were presented with a new code of conduct, the words were unfamiliar, and you struggled to memorize them. Later, of course, you could recite them as easily as you repeat your own name. They – and the lessons they taught – became a part of you.

Tonight, for the first time, you will repeat the Eagle Scout Promise. Again, some of the words will be unfamiliar, but as you live out the life of an Eagle, they too will become a part of you.

Making that new promise does not mean that you should forget all the other promises. Instead, I challenge you to always remember and live by all the promises you've made as a Scout, all the codes you've agreed to follow.

Scoutmaster: Now, finally, it's time for that Eagle Scout Promise we keep talking about. Though the words you say are similar to those you've said so many times before, tonight they will mean more to you than they ever have. When you pledge yourself on your sacred honor, you will be sealing your oath with the words that closed the Declaration of Independence.

I'd like all Eagle Scouts in the audience to stand at this time and rededicate themselves by repeating the Eagle Scout Promise with our new Eagle Scout.

Please make the Scout sign and repeat after me:

> I reaffirm my allegiance
> To the three promises of the Scout Oath.
> I thoughtfully recognize
> And take upon myself
> The obligations and responsibilities
> Of an Eagle Scout.
> On my honor I will do my best
> To make my training and example,
> My rank and my influence
> Count strongly for better Scouting
> And for better citizenship
> In my troop,
> In my community,
> And in my contacts with other people.
> To this I pledge my sacred honor.

Two. *(To Eagles in audience)* Please be seated.

Scoutmaster: Would the honor guard please escort the candidate's parents forward.

(Addressing the honoree) _____, your parents have undoubtedly been your primary source of help and strength.

No one will ever know the unnumbered acts of self-sacrifice from your mother. I'd like your mother to pin the Eagle medal on your uniform. *(She does so.)*

In recognition of your mother's devotion, please present her with this Eagle mother's pin. *(Scout pins on mother's pin.)*

Your father has been the source of much advice and guidance along the Eagle trail, so I'd like him to present the Eagle Scout certificate to you. *(He does so.)*

In return, please present your father with this Eagle lapel pin. *(He does so.)*

(Facing the audience) And now, it gives me great pleasure to present to you our newest Eagle Scout, _____!

(The audience responds with a standing ovation, which you may need to initiate.)

Scoutmaster: We're not through yet, however.

(At this time, any other presentations – from the troop, chartered organization, etc. – are made. The Scoutmaster may also read excerpts from congratulatory letters received. When he is finished, he congratulates the honoree and sits down.)

Closing Period

Master of Ceremonies: Tonight has indeed been a special night. Thank you all for coming out and participating in this wonderful event. Let's give our new Eagle Scout one more round of applause.

I now call on _____ to give our benediction.

Religious Leader or Chaplain Aide: *(Gives benediction.)*

Master of Ceremonies: Again, thank you for coming. Please join us at the reception. Good night.

4. Voice of the Eagle

This ceremony features an off-stage narrator – the Voice of the Eagle – who describes the honoree's history in Scouting and administers the Eagle charge. You can find another version of this ceremony in Troop Program Resources.

In many ways, this ceremony is similar to "Trail to Eagle," although here the Scout's progress through the ranks is demonstrated through a slideshow instead of through his walking down the aisle toward the stage. (See the note about slideshows on page 54.)

As with "Trail to Eagle," it's important that you customize the text in the Eagle segment to fit your honoree.

Opening Period

Master of Ceremonies: Good evening. Tonight we have a special opportunity: to honor Scout _____ as he joins the brotherhood of Eagle Scouts. My name is _____, and I'm
pleased to be serving as your master of ceremonies.

Before we begin our program, I'd like to introduce a few special
people. *(Introduces key troop leaders, representatives of the chartered organization, presenters, and special guests.)*

I'd also like to remind you all that there will be a reception honoring
our new Eagle immediately following the ceremony. *(Other announcements, as necessary, are made here.)*

Now please rise for the invocation, presented by _____,
and remain standing for the presentation of the colors.

Religious Leader or Chaplain Aide: *(Presents an invocation.)*

Scouts: *(Present the colors. One Scout leads the group in the Pledge of Allegiance.)*

Master of Ceremonies: I now call on _____, as a representative of the Boy Scouts of America, to officially convene this court of
honor.

BSA Representative: By the power vested in me by the National Council of the Boy Scouts of America, I declare this court of honor to be duly convened for the sole purpose of presenting the Eagle Scout Award to _____.

Scouting Segment: One Hundred Scouts

Master of Ceremonies: Before we continue with our program tonight, I think it's fitting to pause for a moment and remind ourselves of what Scouting means in the lives of boys – and in the life of our community.

Each Scout brings different needs, interests, and abilities to Scouting, and each takes different lessons away. But research has shown that, by and large, Scouting has an enormous impact on young men's lives. Just listen to these amazing statistics:

Of any 100 boys who become Scouts, it must be confessed that 30 will drop out in their first year. Perhaps this may be regarded as a failure, but in later life all of these will remember that they had been Scouts and will speak well of the program.

Of the 100, only rarely will one ever appear before a juvenile court judge. Twelve of the 100 will be from families who have no religious affiliation. Through Scouting, these 12 and many of their families will be brought into contact with a church, synagogue, or mosque, and will continue to be active all their lives. Six of the 100 will enter the ministry.

Each of the 100 will learn something from Scouting. Almost all will develop hobbies that will add interest throughout the rest of their lives. Many will serve in the military and in varying degrees profit from their Scout training. At least one will use it to save another person's life, and many will credit it with saving their own.

Five of the 100 will reach the rank of Eagle, and at least one will later say that he values his Eagle badge above his college degree. Many will find their future vocation through merit-badge work and Scouting contacts. Seventeen of the 100 boys will later become Scout leaders and will give leadership to thousands of additional boys.

Only one in four boys in America will become a Scout, but it is interesting to know that of the leaders of this nation in business, religion, and politics, three out of four were Scouts.

Tonight, of course, we're here to honor not a hundred Scouts, but just one. In a moment, we'll hear about some of the things he's learned in Scouting. While we know the things he has done in the past, we can only imagine what he'll do in the future.

Eagle Segment: Voice of the Eagle

Master of Ceremonies: Will the honor guard please escort the candidate forward. *(The honor guard consists of two or three Scouts, either Eagles, soon-to-be Eagles, or members of the honoree's patrol. The honoree is seated on stage, and the other Scouts return to their seats.)*

(At this point, the lights are dimmed, and the Voice of the Eagle begins to speak. A slideshow of pictures of the honoree corresponds with the text.)

Voice of the Eagle: This is the Voice of the Eagle, the Eagle who has watched for years as you've struggled to ascend to our aerie.

Think back for a moment, back to the day when you first joined Troop ____. How small you felt in your crisp new uniform, struggling to recite the Scout Oath and Scout Law with the other Scouts. I watched as you stole a glance upward, looking toward the clouds and wondering if you could ever achieve the summit of Scouting.

Soon, you began to advance, mastering the Oath and the Law and beginning to learn the ways of the Scout. You camped overnight and then for a weekend – and then spent an entire week away from home at summer camp. I watched you grow that week in skills and in spirit, and I saw the pride on your face as the Scoutmaster handed you your Tenderfoot badge.

It wasn't long before a year had passed. Your Tenderfoot badge was long gone, replaced by the Second Class badge and then by the badge of the First Class Scout. You had begun in earnest the climb toward Eagle, and as I watched, I could sense your determination.

But I also knew that many Scouts start off determined, only to become discouraged. For the climb from First Class to Eagle becomes harder with each step, and only a handful of Scouts reach the top. In fact, as you climbed, you could see that there were far fewer Scouts ahead of you, clearing the path, than there behind you, following in your footsteps.

Along the way, I watched you grow in other ways in Scouting. *(Briefly describes the honoree's camp staff experience, Order of the Arrow membership, or participation in a national jamboree or other high-adventure activity.)*

Then, finally, on _____, you broke through the clouds and became a Life Scout. Now, I could see clearly into your face and your heart, and I knew that someday you would join our Eagle brotherhood.

Over these past months, I've watched as you've earned the last of your merit badges, so that now ___ badges parade across your sash. I've watched you serve our troop as *(leadership position)*, reaching down constantly to help your fellow Scouts in their climb toward the summit. And I've watched you give back to your community through your Eagle Scout service project. *(Briefly describes the Scout's Eagle service project.)*

Now, I stand ready – with all the Eagles who have gone before you – to welcome you to our aerie as you join the brotherhood of Eagle Scouts.

The Presentation of the Eagle Badge

(The slideshow ends, the lights come up, and the master of ceremonies returns to the microphone.)

Master of Ceremonies: It's now time for the highlight of our program: the presentation of the Eagle Scout Award. I'd like to ask Scoutmaster _____ to come forward to make the appropriate presentations.

Scoutmaster: We have heard a lot tonight about what it means to be an Eagle Scout. Now our honoree will have the chance to tell us a little about what being an Eagle Scout means to him.

Honoree: *(Talks about what he's learned in the program, what the highlights of his time in Scouting have been, and what being an Eagle means to him. If the Scout wants to give the Scoutmaster or a mentor a gift, this would be an appropriate time.)*

Scoutmaster: Becoming an Eagle Scout is a great honor; it's also a great responsibility. At this time, the Voice of the Eagle will remind you of what it means to live as an Eagle Scout.

Voice of the Eagle: As an Eagle Scout, I'm pleased to welcome you to the brotherhood of Eagle Scouts. Only five percent of the boys who enter Scouting achieve what you have here tonight. Your achievement is recognition of your perseverance and ability.

But I am not here to talk of your past accomplishments, which are great, but of your future opportunities. Of course, when you go to a Scouting function, you will be recognized as a doer, and you will have the opportunity of standing as a leader among leaders.

But your Eagle award will have meaning far beyond Scouting itself. You are a marked man, and your achievement will follow you throughout your life. The things you have done, the leadership and sense of honor you have developed will mean more to you than a certificate and a piece of ribbon. You will have more opportunity to be of service to your fellow man through your school, your work, and through Scouting, because you know what you can do.

In the years to come, you will casually meet people who are Eagles too, and there will be an instant bond of comradeship. You have each shared a common experience; you each know that the other can be trusted. The comradeship among Eagles extends throughout the world of Scouting and into the larger world beyond. For the rest of your life, you travel as a marked man, an Eagle Scout. Welcome!

(At this point, the Voice of the Eagle – especially if he is a special person in the Eagle's life – may enter and personally congratulate the honoree.)

Scoutmaster: Many times over the last few years, you've joined with your fellow Scouts in repeating the Scout Oath. Now, you will stand alone and repeat a new oath, the Eagle Scout Promise. Though the words you say are similar to those you've said so many times before, tonight they will mean more to you than they ever have. When you pledge yourself on your sacred honor, you will be sealing your oath with the words that closed the Declaration of Independence.

I'd like all Eagle Scouts in the audience to stand at this time and rededicate themselves by repeating the Eagle Scout Promise with our new Eagle Scout.

Please make the Scout sign and repeat after me:

> I reaffirm my allegiance
> To the three promises of the Scout Oath.
> I thoughtfully recognize
> And take upon myself
> The obligations and responsibilities
> Of an Eagle Scout.
> On my honor I will do my best
> To make my training and example,
> My rank and my influence
> Count strongly for better Scouting
> And for better citizenship
> In my troop,
> In my community,
> And in my contacts with other people.
> To this I pledge my sacred honor.

Two. *(To Eagles in audience)* Please be seated.

Scoutmaster: Would the honor guard please escort the candidate's parents forward.

(Addressing the honoree) _____, your parents have undoubtedly been your primary source of help and strength.

No one will ever know the unnumbered acts of self-sacrifice from your mother. I'd like your mother to pin the Eagle medal on your uniform. *(She does so.)*

In recognition of your mother's devotion, please present her with this Eagle mother's pin. *(Scout pins on mother's pin.)*

Your father has been the source of much advice and guidance along the Eagle trail, so I'd like him to present the Eagle Scout certificate to you. *(He does so.)*

In return, please present your father with this Eagle lapel pin. *(He does so.)*

(Facing the audience) And now, it gives me great pleasure to present to you our newest Eagle Scout, _____!

(The audience responds with a standing ovation, which you may need to initiate.)

Scoutmaster: We're not through yet, however.

(At this time, any other presentations – from the troop, chartered organization, etc. – are made. The Scoutmaster may also read excerpts from congratulatory letters received. When he is finished, he congratulates the honoree and sits down.)

Closing Period

Master of Ceremonies: Tonight has indeed been a special night. Thank you all for coming out and participating in this wonderful event. Let's give our new Eagle Scout one more round of applause.

I now call on _____ to give our benediction.

Religious Leader or Chaplain Aide: *(Gives benediction.)*

Master of Ceremonies: Again, thank you for coming. Please join us at the reception. Good night.

5. The Challenge

"The Challenge" is reminiscent of the days when the term "court of honor" referred to what we now call a board of review, the meeting where a Scout is examined and judged worthy of his next rank. During the Eagle segment of this ceremony, three audience members rise to "challenge" the honoree before he receives the Eagle badge.

It's important to strike just the right tone with this ceremony. Don't be too serious about the challenges, but also don't let the whole thing turn into a comedy. Also, be sure the Scout and his family know what is going on and aren't surprised when people stand up and challenge him.

Opening Period

Master of Ceremonies: Good evening. My name is _____, and I'm pleased to serve as master of ceremonies on this special occasion. ___ years ago, Scout _____ accepted a challenge – not only to learn the Scout Oath and Law, but to live them out in his daily life, not only to be a good Scout, but to become one of the best, one of the five percent of all Scouts worthy of the rank of Eagle. Since that time, he has successfully met that challenge, and we are gathered here tonight to celebrate his achievement.

Before we begin our program, I'd like to introduce a few special people. *(Introduces key troop leaders, representatives of the chartered organization, presenters, and special guests.)*

I'd like to remind you all that there will be a reception honoring our new Eagle immediately following the ceremony. *(Other announcements, as necessary, are made here.)*

Now please rise for the invocation, presented by _____, and remain standing for the presentation of the colors.

Religious Leader or Chaplain Aide: *(Presents an invocation.)*

Scouts: *(Present the colors. One Scout leads the group in the Pledge of Allegiance.)*

Master of Ceremonies: I now call on _____, as a representative of the Boy Scouts of America, to officially convene this court of honor.

BSA Representative: By the power vested in me by the National Council of the Boy Scouts of America, I declare this court of honor to be duly convened for the sole purpose of presenting the Eagle Scout Award to _____.

Scouting Segment: Scout Oath Rededication

Master of Ceremonies: Before we continue with our program, I think it's appropriate for all the Scouts and Scouters in the room to rededicate themselves to the principles of Scouting by reciting together the Scout Oath. Would all Scouts and Scouters please stand.

Scout sign. *(Leads Scout Oath.)* Thank you. Please be seated.

Eagle Segment: The Challenge

(The First Class Scout, Life Scout, and Eagle Scout who participate in this segment should be seated in different places throughout the audience. They should have their lines memorized.)

Master of Ceremonies: It's now time for the highlight of our program: the presentation of the Eagle Scout Award. I'd like to ask Scoutmaster _____ to come forward to make the appropriate presentations.

Scoutmaster: Will the honor guard please escort the candidate forward. *(The honor guard consists of two or three Scouts, either Eagles, soon-to-be Eagles, or members of the honoree's patrol.)*

Awarding the Eagle Scout badge is an important and serious matter. It is a goal toward which this Scout has been working for many years and is the culmination of the efforts of his parents and Scout leaders. This is an occasion for pride and for joy, but also a time for serious contemplation.

(Addressing the honoree) _____, a few moments ago, you joined with your fellow Scouts in repeating the Scout Oath, words you've repeated many, many times. Shortly, you will stand alone and repeat a new oath, the Eagle Scout Promise. Though the words you say are similar to those you've said so many times before, tonight they will mean more to you than they ever have. When you pledge yourself on your sacred honor, you will be sealing your oath with the words that closed the Declaration of Independence.

I will read the Eagle Scout Promise to you now so that you will know what you are about to pledge, and I will then ask you to repeat it after me.

I reaffirm my allegiance to the three promises of the Scout Oath. I thoughtfully recognize and take upon myself the obligations and responsibilities of an Eagle Scout. On my honor I will do my best to make my training and example, my rank and my influence count strongly for better Scouting and for better citizenship in my troop, in my community, and in my contacts with other people. To this I pledge my sacred honor.

Having heard the Eagle Scout Promise, are you willing to adopt it?

Honoree: I am.

Scoutmaster: Please make the Scout sign and repeat after me.

First Class Scout: *(Rising to his feet)* Stop! I challenge the right of this Scout to be awarded the rank of Eagle!

Scoutmaster: Who are you and by what right do you challenge?

First Class Scout: I am a First Class Scout, and the respect I have for the uniform I wear gives me the right to so challenge.

Scoutmaster: What is the nature of your challenge?

First Class Scout: As a First Class Scout, I have mastered the basic skills of Scouting. Has this Scout attained the necessary skills to become an Eagle Scout?

Scoutmaster: As Scoutmaster of Troop _____, I certify that this Scout attained the rank of First Class on _____. Since that time, he has earned ___ merit badges, including all of those required for Eagle. He has demonstrated that he does indeed possess the skills of an Eagle Scout. Are you now satisfied?

First Class Scout: I am. *(He sits down.)*

Life Scout: *(Rising to his feet)* I, too, challenge the right of this Scout to be awarded the rank of Eagle.

Scoutmaster: Who are you and by what right do you challenge?

Life Scout: I am a Life Scout, and my esteem for the Eagle rank gives me the right to so challenge.

Scoutmaster: What is the nature of your challenge?

Life Scout: As a Life Scout, service and leadership are my watchwords. Has this Scout satisfactorily completed the service and leadership requirements of the Eagle rank?

Scoutmaster: He has. He has led the troop as *(leadership position held)* for a period of six months and has served his community by (briefly describes the Scout's Eagle service project). Are you now satisfied?

Life Scout: I am. *(He sits down.)*

Eagle Scout: *(Rising to his feet)* I, too, challenge the right of this Scout to be awarded the rank of Eagle.

Scoutmaster: Who are you and by what right do you challenge?

Eagle Scout: I am an Eagle Scout, and the badge I wear over my heart gives me the right to so challenge.

Scoutmaster: What is the nature of your challenge?

Eagle Scout: Has this Scout, now nearing the end of the Eagle trail, demonstrated his willingness and ability to live and act in accordance with the ideals of Scouting, as exemplified by the Scout Oath, Law, Motto, and Slogan?

BSA Representative: As a representative of the Boy Scouts of America, I certify that the Eagle Scout board of review, after thorough investigation, interview, and examination, has concluded unanimously that this Scout has demonstrated his willingness and ability to live out the spirit of Scouting in his daily life.

Scoutmaster: Are you now satisfied?

Eagle Scout: Still, I am not satisfied. I believe that this candidate should understand that the Eagle badge is a mark of responsibility as well as one of honor. I respectfully ask that this candidate be informed of the responsibilities of an Eagle Scout before continuing further.

Scoutmaster: I agree. And I feel that no one is more qualified to impart this knowledge than one who already wears the Eagle badge. At this time, I would ask Eagle Scout _____ to outline the responsibilities of the Eagle. *(Eagle Scout in audience sits down.)*

"Charger": *(Addressing the honoree)* Becoming an Eagle Scout is a great accomplishment; being an Eagle Scout is a great responsibility. As an Eagle, the Scout Oath and Scout Law should take on new meaning for you; the motto and slogan take on new urgency.

As an Eagle, your first obligation is to live with honor. You are a marked man, a leader; for good or ill, people will follow the example you set. Give up anything before you give up your reputation and good name. As Shakespeare said, "Mine honor is my life; both grow in one. Take honor from me, and my life is done." Let the white of the Eagle badge remind you of honor.

Your second obligation as an Eagle Scout is to be loyal. As a follower, you promised to be loyal to those above you. Now, as a leader, you must also be loyal to those below you, treating them as you would want to be treated. And you must also be loyal to your ideals, not letting others sway you from your course. Let the blue of the Eagle badge remind you of loyalty.

Your third obligation as an Eagle Scout is to be courageous. Stepping into your new role as a leader, you will face many challenges and obstacles. A ship in the harbor is safe, but that's not what ships are for. You must have the courage to do what is right, whatever other people do or say. Let the red of the Eagle badge remind you of courage.

Your fourth obligation is to serve others, for a leader is above all a servant. Let the practice of the daily good turn become a lifetime of service, for only in giving of yourself do you give anything of value.

Just as it always has, let the scroll on your badge remind you of service.

Your final obligation as an Eagle Scout is to have vision. As a leader, you must now blaze your own trail. Just as a bald eagle soaring high above the ground can look far into the distance, so too must you look far into the future. Many people will follow you; only with vision will you lead them in the right direction. Let the silver eagle hanging from your badge reminds you of vision.

These then are your obligations as an Eagle Scout: honor, loyalty, courage, service, and vision. By meeting those obligations, you can lead your troop, your community, your nation toward a better tomorrow.

Eagle Scout: *(Rising to his feet)* Mr. Scoutmaster, if this candidate is willing and eager to accept the mantle of responsibility as well as the honor of the badge, then I will be satisfied and will request that you proceed to administer the Eagle Scout Promise.

Scoutmaster: *(Addressing the honoree)* Are you ready and willing to accept these responsibilities and to adopt the Eagle Scout Promise I read to you earlier?

Honoree: I am.

Scoutmaster: I'd like all Eagle Scouts in the audience to stand at this time and rededicate themselves by repeating the Eagle Scout Promise with our new Eagle Scout.

Please make the Scout sign and repeat after me:

> I reaffirm my allegiance
> To the three promises of the Scout Oath.
> I thoughtfully recognize
> And take upon myself
> The obligations and responsibilities
> Of an Eagle Scout.

On my honor I will do my best
To make my training and example,
My rank and my influence
Count strongly for better Scouting
And for better citizenship
In my troop,
In my community,
And in my contacts with other people.
To this I pledge my sacred honor.

Two. *(To Eagles in audience)* Please be seated.

The Presentation of the Eagle Badge

Scoutmaster: Would the honor guard please escort the candidate's parents forward.

(Addressing the honoree) _____, your parents have undoubtedly been your primary source of help and strength.

No one will ever know the unnumbered acts of self-sacrifice from your mother. I'd like your mother to pin the Eagle medal on your uniform. *(She does so.)*

In recognition of your mother's devotion, please present her with this Eagle mother's pin. *(Scout pins on mother's pin.)*

Your father has been the source of much advice and guidance along the Eagle trail, so I'd like him to present the Eagle Scout certificate to you. *(He does so.)*

In return, please present your father with this Eagle lapel pin. *(He does so.)*

(Facing the audience) And now, it gives me great pleasure to present to you our newest Eagle Scout, _____!

(The audience responds with a standing ovation, which you may need to initiate.)

Scoutmaster: We're not through yet, however.

(At this time, any other presentations – from the troop, chartered organization, etc. – are made. The Scoutmaster may also read excerpts from congratulatory letters received. When he is finished, he congratulates the honoree and sits down.)

Closing Period

Master of Ceremonies: Tonight has indeed been a special night. Scout _____ has accepted a weighty challenge: to live out the Eagle Scout Promise in his everyday life. It's a challenge worthy of each of us. Let's give our new Eagle Scout one more round of applause.

I now call on _____ to give our benediction.

Religious Leader or Chaplain Aide: *(Gives benediction.)*

Master of Ceremonies: Again, thank you for coming. Please join us at the reception. Good night.

6. Order of the Arrow

If the honoree is active in the Order of the Arrow, the following ceremony is especially appropriate. It involves characters reminiscent of OA ceremonies and hearkens back to the traditions of the Order – without, of course, revealing any secrets to nonmembers or making those nonmembers feel left out or uncomfortable.

The Tribal Chief, the Guide, and the Four Winds should be in ceremonial attire. The room should be decorated appropriately.

Opening Period

Tribal Chief: I am the Tribal Chief, and I welcome you as we open our lodge for this special ceremony. Tonight we honor one who has excelled as a Scout and as an Arrowman, a young man who has reached the pinnacle of Scouting by attaining the rank of Eagle Scout. This is a great moment worthy of celebration.

Before we begin our ceremony, several of our number deserve special recognition. *(Introduces key troop leaders, representatives of the chartered organization, presenters, and special guests.)*

To further honor our new Eagle Scout, I invite each of you to a special reception immediately following the ceremony. *(Other announcements, as necessary, are made here.)*

Now, as we are all one nation and live under one God, please rise for the invocation, presented by _____, and remain standing for the presentation of the colors.

Religious Leader or Chaplain Aide: *(Presents an invocation.)*

Scouts: *(Present the colors. One Scout leads the group in the Pledge of Allegiance.)*

Tribal Chief: I now call on _____, as a representative of the Boy Scouts of America, to officially convene this court of honor.

BSA Representative: By the power vested in me by the National Council of the Boy Scouts of America, I declare this court of honor to be duly convened for the sole purpose of presenting the Eagle Scout Award to _____.

Scouting Segment: The Four Winds

(A slow, steady drumbeat is heard from a distance. The Four Winds enter slowly from the rear and move to the north, south, east, and west corners of the room. The drumbeat ends.)

Tribal Chief: As Scouts, we are bound together in brotherhood by the Scout Law, a sacred set of principles for living whose origins are lost in the mist of time. Listen now to the wisdom of the winds.

(At the front of the room is a candelabrum with 12 candles, representing the points of the Scout Law. As each of the Four Winds recites a point of the Scout Law, a uniformed Scout lights a candle.)

East Wind: I am the spirit of the East Wind. I represent the common law, a Scout's duty to God and to country. Trustworthy, loyal, and helpful are the qualities that a man must possess who lives by the laws of this land. The Scout must be always worthy of his brother's trust and show loyalty to all to whom it is due. May the daily good turn be a central focus of your life.

West Wind: As the spirit of the West Wind, I represent the law of equity, your duty to country and to others. Friendly, courteous, and kind are the principles that speak of conscience. They create the atmosphere that comes from within your heart. Kindle the desire to be a friend to those of all ages and stations in life. Be courteous to those whom you pass along the trail. Cast away the harmful spirits of unfriendliness and selfishness.

South Wind: I am the spirit of the South Wind. I represent civil law, your duty to others and to self. Obedient, cheerful, and thrifty are the marks of civility. Obedience is something we all must learn, to take orders and carry them out cheerfully. Real thrift means spending both money and time wisely and sharing both with those less fortunate than us.

North Wind: I am the spirit of the North Wind, the most powerful of all. I represent the divine law, your duty to be brave and clean and reverent. To be brave is to be unselfish in service, always prepared to face the unknown. Cast from your mind and body any unclean spirits that try to weaken or destroy you. Live a life of reverence toward God.

(The drumbeats resume and the Four Winds depart.)

Eagle Segment: The Challenge

(As the drumbeats continue, the Guide and the honoree appear at the rear of the room and walk slowly forward to face the Tribal Chief, who stands just outside the presentation area. When they stop, the drumbeats end. The Guide taps the Tribal Chief on the right shoulder, giving three long taps. The Tribal Chief responds with one long and two short taps on the Guide's right shoulder.)

Tribal Chief: Brother Guide, who is this person who seeks admission into our circle?

The Guide: He is _____, a young man who believes himself worthy to wear the mark of the Eagle.

Tribal Chief: Is there one here who can vouch for him?

Scoutmaster: I am a _____, Scoutmaster of Troop ___, and I can vouch for this young man and his abilities. It is only right that he be admitted to the Eagle brotherhood.

Tribal Chief: To wear the wings of the Eagle, a young man must pass many seasons in his troop and must live out the principles of Scouting in his everyday life. Has this young man done so?

Scoutmaster: He has. Since becoming a Life Scout on _____ _____, he has participated actively in the meetings and outings of the troop. He has shown that the spirit of Scouting is alive within him.

Tribal Chief: To enter the Eagle aerie, a Scout must earn at least 21 merit badges, mastering the skills of Scouting and exploring those career and hobby interests that he chooses. Has this young man done so?

Scoutmaster: He has. He has earned a total of ___ merit badges, including all of those required for Eagle.

Tribal Chief: To become a member of the Eagle brotherhood, a young man must serve his fellows by leading them. Has this young man done so?

Scoutmaster: He has. Since becoming a Life Scout, he has served as *(leadership position held)*, leading his brother Scouts toward a better tomorrow.

Tribal Chief: And finally, to become an Eagle Scout, a young man must serve his community through a special project, working gladly, not begrudgingly, in faithfulness to the principles of Scouting. Has this young man done so?

Scoutmaster: He has. *(Briefly describes the Scout's Eagle service project.)*

Tribal Chief: I am satisfied that _____ has met the challenges of the Eagle without flinching. Brother Guide, you may bring the candidate into our circle.

The Presentation of the Eagle Badge

Tribal Chief: We have heard much tonight about what it means to be an Eagle Scout. Now I would ask _____ to tell us a little about what being an Eagle Scout means to him.

Honoree: *(Talks about what he's learned in the program, what the highlights of his time in Scouting have been, and what being an Eagle means to him. If the Scout wants to give the Scoutmaster or a mentor a gift, this would be an appropriate time.)*

Tribal Chief: *(Addressing the honoree)* Tonight you join the brotherhood of Eagle Scouts. Much as you did when you joined our Order and first wore the Arrow, you are being honored not so much for what you have done, but for what you will do in the future. As you did at our council fire many seasons ago, you are committing yourself to a life of cheerful service and righteous living.

Brother Guide will remind you of what is required of an Eagle Scout, using the teachings of Wabasha as his guide.

The Guide: Hear the words of Wabasha and heed them: When you arise in the morning, give thanks for the morning light. Give thanks for your life and strength, for your food and for the joy of living. Be merciful to those who are in your power; it is the part of a chief to take care of the weak, the sick, the old and the helpless. Show respect to all men, but grovel to none. Remember: a man is bound by his promise with a bond that cannot be broken. Be hospitable. Be kind. A man tried and proven is at all times clean, courteous, and master of himself. Thus spoke a great chief, and thus you must do.

Also remember the words of the East Wind, who urged you to be trustworthy, loyal, and helpful; the West Wind, who told you to be friendly, courteous, and kind; the words of the South Wind, who reminded you to be obedient, cheerful, and thrifty; and finally, the words of the North Wind, the most powerful of all, who admonished you to be brave, clean, and reverent.

Tribal Chief: My brother, for now I am permitted to hail you by this endearing title, I ask that take upon yourself the solemn obligations of the Eagle by repeating the Eagle Scout Promise. Though the words you say are similar to those you've said so many times before, tonight they will mean more to you than they ever have.

I would ask all Eagle Scouts in the audience to stand at this time and rededicate themselves by repeating the Eagle Scout Promise with our new Eagle Scout.

Please make the Scout sign and repeat after me:

> I reaffirm my allegiance
> To the three promises of the Scout Oath.
> I thoughtfully recognize
> And take upon myself
> The obligations and responsibilities
> Of an Eagle Scout.

On my honor I will do my best
To make my training and example,
My rank and my influence
Count strongly for better Scouting
And for better citizenship
In my troop,
In my community,
And in my contacts with other people.
To this I pledge my sacred honor.

Two. *(To Eagles in audience)* Please be seated.

Tribal Chief: Brother Guide, please escort the candidate's parents forward.

(Addressing the honoree) _____, your parents have undoubtedly been your primary source of help and strength as you've journeyed along the Eagle trail.

No one will ever know the unnumbered acts of self-sacrifice from your mother. I would ask your mother to pin the Eagle medal on your uniform. *(She does so.)*

In recognition of your mother's devotion, please present her with this Eagle mother's pin. *(Scout pins on mother's pin.)*

Your father has been the source of much advice and guidance, so I would ask him to present the Eagle Scout certificate to you. *(He does so.)*

In return, please present your father with this Eagle lapel pin. *(He does so.)*

(Facing the audience) And now, it gives me great pleasure to present to you Eagle Scout _____!

(The audience responds with a standing ovation, which you may need to initiate.)

Now, I would ask Scoutmaster _____ to make any additional presentations.

(At this time, any other presentations – from the troop, chartered organization, etc. – are made. The Scoutmaster may also read excerpts from congratulatory letters received. When he is finished, he congratulates the honoree and sits down.)

Closing Period

Tribal Chief: The eagle is strong and powerful. He flies unblinking into the face of the sun. He soars high and builds his nest on a pinnacle. Tonight, we have welcomed Scout _____ into the brotherhood of Eagles. Thank you all for participating in this special event. Let's give our new Eagle Scout one more round of applause. I now call on _____ to give our benediction.

Religious Leader or Chaplain Aide: *(Gives benediction.)*

Tribal Chief: Again, thank you for coming; I invite you to join us at the reception. I now declare this council meeting closed. Good night.

7. Late Night

Most Eagle courts of honor are pretty formal affairs. That's usually okay, but some honorees would prefer more laid-back ceremonies. With a nod to generations of late-night television hosts, this script fills that need. It also demonstrates a simple way to include multiple honorees. This ceremony works best when nearly all the presenter are current or recent Scouts who understand the late-night vibe and can adapt the script to fit their personalities. If possible, recruit a small stage band that can play during lulls in the program and provide rim shots for jokes.

Create a late-show set with an anchor desk for the master of ceremonies (dubbed the host here) and a couch for his sidekick (the straight man some television hosts have) and the honorees. The band should be on one side. The awards should be laid out on a table on the other side. Only the band should be on stage at first.

Opening Period

Off-stage Announcer: Good evening, ladies and gentlemen, and welcome to Troop _____ Live! We've got a great show lined up for you tonight, but first, here's a message from your senior patrol leader, _____.

Senior Patrol Leader: Please rise for the invocation, presented by _____, and remain standing for the presentation of the colors, the Pledge of Allegiance, and the Scout Oath.

Religious Leader or Chaplain Aide: *(Presents an invocation.)*

Scouts: *(Present the colors. One Scout leads the group in the Pledge of Allegiance and the Scout Oath.)*

Off-stage Announcer: Thank you very much, _____. Now, let's get this show on the road. With further ado, here's a man who needs no introduction, your host, _____!

Host *(entering from off-stage)*: Good evening, everybody, and thanks for that great introduction. Oh, wait. You really didn't introduce me. *(Briefly tells about himself, something like "I'm a Troop _____ Eagle Scout and currently serve as an assistant Scoutmaster when I'm home from college.")* But enough about me. We do have a great show tonight because we will be meeting not one, not three, but two brand-new Eagle Scouts, _____ and _____.

Scouting Segment: What the Scout Oath Means to Me

(If possible, replace the definitions of the parts of the Scout Oath in this section with definitions written by members of the troop. Change the introductory text as appropriate.)

Host: Before we do that, however, I want to talk about this Scout Oath thing. I heard you all recite it, but I'm not sure you get what it means. Hey, _____, come up here and educate these folks.

Sidekick: Sure thing. So I wasn't real sure about some of the big words in there....

Host: Big words?

Sidekick: Yeah. Some of them even have three syllables.

Host: Wow!

Sidekick: Yeah, so I looked up some stuff about the Scout Oath and found where this one Scout explained what the Scout Oath meant to him. So you say a line from the Scout Oath, and I'll tell you what it means. Ready?

Host: Sure.

Sidekick: Set?

Host: Let's get on with it.

Sidekick: Go!

Host: A Scout is trustworthy.

Sidekick: Umm, I think that's the Scout Law.

Host: Oh, yeah. My bad. On my honor.

Sidekick: Meaning your solemn promise; a promise that relies on your good reputation as to whether or not it will be carried out.

Host: I will do my best.

Sidekick: Your best? What is it? It's giving it all you've got when you've got something to do – and working on it with all your heart and soul and mind, all the strength and devotion you've got. Then you're doing your best.

Host: To do my duty.

Sidekick: To do the job; to meet the responsibilities; to do what has to be done – not just halfway, not just half a job, but completely – completely and fully so that you're proud of your work.

Host: To God and my country.

Sidekick: Duty to whom? First, to God. Fulfill your religious responsibilities; uphold your religious beliefs. Second, to your country. I know you've been told how lucky you are to live in a free country. I hope that you are aware of it. Being told and being aware are two different things. And I hope that you will soon be aware of the responsibility you have to your country – your duty.

Host: To obey the Scout Law.

Sidekick: Meaning to obey it, to follow it completely, not just halfway. And not just the first six points or the last three or every other one, but all twelve points, at all times.

Host: To help other people at all times.

Sidekick: To help ... it doesn't say much. It could mean saving a life or changing a tire or carrying a bag of groceries. To help other people, not just your family. And at all times, not just when it is convenient for you or when your Scoutmaster is watching – but at all times. And the best time is when you have to go out of your way to do it.

Host: To keep myself physically strong.

Sidekick: Just what it says – physically strong; ready to defend yourself, your Scouting principles, your country.

Host: Mentally awake.

Sidekick: Keep alert, observing, always trying to learn.

Host: And morally straight.

Sidekick: In thought and actions, decide what is right and what is wrong and stand by the right. The end.

Host: Thanks, dude. That was great. By the way, do you know what the Scout neckerchief said to the Scout cap?

Sidekick: No, I don't. What did the Scout neckerchief say to the Scout cap?

Host: You go on ahead. I'll hang around here.

Sidekick: Ouch! Maybe we'd better get on with the show.

Host: Yeah, maybe we'd better.

Eagle Segment: Q&A

Host: Like I said at the top of the show, we have two very special guests this evening, Troop _____'s two newest Eagle Scouts, _____ and _____. Before we invite them up, I'd like Senior Patrol Leader _____ to tell us a little more about _____ *(first honoree)*.

Senior Patrol Leader: *(Presents a brief summary of the honoree's Scouting history. This shouldn't be a dry summary of badges earned and offices held. Instead, tell some interesting things the boy has done, focusing on his growth in Scouting.)*

Host: Thanks, _____. Now, put your hands together for _____ *(first honoree)*.

(First honoree comes on stage and sits on the couch. The sidekick moves down to give him space. The host and sidekick interview the first honoree for a few minutes. The topics should be customized based on the individual, but they could include his Eagle Scout service project, his favorite Scouting

memories, his most embarrassing moment, the origin of his nickname, or his college plans.)

Host: It's been great chatting with you, _____. We've put together a little video about your time in Scouting. Feast your eyes on this.

(An off-stage leader plays a video tracing the first honoree's time in Scouting.)

Host: Very nice. Now, let's get _____ *(senior patrol leader)* to tell us about our second guest.

Senior Patrol Leader: *(As before, presents a brief summary of the honoree's Scouting history.)*

Host: Now, give it up for our second new Eagle Scout, _____ *(second honoree).*

(Second honoree comes on stage and sits on the couch. The first honoree and the sidekick move down to give him space. As before, the host and sidekick interview the second honoree. While some of the questions may be the same, a few should be different to keep the segment fresh.)

Host: No big surprise, but we've got a little video to show you, too.

(An off-stage leader plays a video tracing the second honoree's time in Scouting.)

Host: Awesome. It's certainly been fun getting to know you guys a little better. Now, it's time for the moment you've all been waiting for. Scoutmaster _____ is going to take over the show and hand out a little Boy Scout bling.

The Presentation of the Eagle Badge

(If the stage is large enough, this part of the ceremony should take place off to the side, away from the late-show set. When it comes time to hand out medals and pins, things happen simultaneously . Both mothers pin the

badges on at the same time, both honorees pin their mothers at the same time, etc.)

Scoutmaster: *(To the host)* Thanks for a great show, _____ *(To the honorees)* Guys, please join me over here. This has been a fun evening, but now we come to the serious part. By becoming Eagle Scouts, you are taking on some serious responsibilities. I'd like _____ to talk about that.

"Charger": Becoming an Eagle Scout is a great accomplishment; being an Eagle Scout is a great responsibility. As an Eagle, the Scout Oath and Scout Law should take on new meaning for you; the motto and slogan take on new urgency.

As an Eagle, your first obligation is to live with honor. You are a marked man, a leader; for good or ill, people will follow the example you set. Give up anything before you give up your reputation and good name. As Shakespeare said, "Mine honor is my life; both grow in one. Take honor from me, and my life is done." Let the white of the Eagle badge remind you of honor.

Your second obligation as an Eagle Scout is to be loyal. As a follower, you promised to be loyal to those above you. Now, as a leader, you must also be loyal to those below you, treating them as you would want to be treated. And you must also be loyal to your ideals, not letting others sway you from your course. Let the blue of the Eagle badge remind you of loyalty.

Your third obligation as an Eagle Scout is to be courageous. Stepping into your new role as a leader, you will face many challenges and obstacles. A ship in the harbor is safe, but that's not what ships are for. You must have the courage to do what is right, no matter what other people do or say. Let the red of the Eagle badge remind you of courage.

Your fourth obligation is to serve others, for a leader is above all a servant. Let the practice of the daily good turn lead to a lifetime of service, for only in giving of yourself do you give anything of value.

Just as it always has, let the scroll on your badge remind you of service.

Your final obligation as an Eagle Scout is to have vision. As a leader, you must now blaze your own trail. Just as a bald eagle soaring high above the ground can look far into the distance, so too must you look far into the future. Many people will follow you; only with vision will you lead them in the right direction. Let the silver eagle hanging from your badge remind you of vision.

These then are your obligations as an Eagle Scout: honor, loyalty, courage, service, and vision. By meeting these obligations, you can lead your troop, your community, your nation toward a better tomorrow.

Scoutmaster: Guys, many times over the last few years, you've joined with your fellow Scouts in repeating the Scout Oath. Now, you will stand alone and repeat a new oath, the Eagle Scout Promise. Though the words you say are similar to those you've said so many times before, tonight they will mean more to you than they ever have. When you pledge yourselves on your sacred honor, you will be sealing your oath with the words that closed the Declaration of Independence.

I'd like all Eagle Scouts in the audience to stand at this time and rededicate themselves by repeating the Eagle Scout Promise with our new Eagle Scouts.

Please make the Scout sign and repeat after me:

> I reaffirm my allegiance
> To the three promises of the Scout Oath.
> I thoughtfully recognize
> And take upon myself
> The obligations and responsibilities
> Of an Eagle Scout.
> On my honor I will do my best
> To make my training and example,
> My rank and my influence

Count strongly for better Scouting
And for better citizenship
In my troop,
In my community,
And in my contacts with other people.
To this I pledge my sacred honor.

Two. *(To Eagles in audience)* Please be seated.

Scoutmaster: Would the honor guard please escort the candidates' parents forward. *(The honor guard for each honoree consists of two or three Scouts, either Eagles, soon-to-be Eagles, or members of his patrol.)*

(Addressing the honorees) _____, your parents have undoubtedly been your primary source of help and strength.

No one will ever know the unnumbered acts of self-sacrifice from your mothers. I'd like your mothers to pin the Eagle medal on your uniforms. *(They do so.)*

In recognition of your mothers' devotion, please present them with the Eagle mother's pin. *(Scouts pin on mother's pins.)*

Your fathers have been the source of much advice and guidance along the Eagle trail, so I'd like them to present the Eagle Scout certificate to you. *(They do so.)*

In return, please present your fathers with the Eagle lapel pin. *(They do so.)*

(Facing the audience) And now, it gives me great pleasure to present to you our newest Eagle Scouts, _____ and _____!

(The audience responds with a standing ovation, which you may need to initiate. Given the theme of this ceremony, you could even have a Scout hold up a big sign that says "Applause.")

Scoutmaster: We're not through yet, however.

*(At this time, any other presentations – from the troop, chartered orga-
nization, etc. – are made. The Scoutmaster may also read excerpts from
congratulatory letters received. When he is finished, he congratulates the
honoree and sits down.)*

Closing Period

Host: Thank you, Scoutmaster _____. Well, it looks like our time is
almost up. I'd like to call on _____ to give our benediction. After that, please join us for the after-party.

Religious Leader or Chaplain Aide: *(Gives benediction.)*

8. College and Career

*Most Eagle Scouts receive their Eagle badges during, or perhaps shortly after,
high school. Occasionally, however, an honoree comes back from college or military service to receive his Eagle badge. Such an honoree is no less deserving of a
court of honor, but his ceremony should have a somewhat different flavor than
other ceremonies. This script serves as a good starting point. Note that it uses
fewer presenters than usual and could easily be conducted in someone's home.*

Opening Period

Master of Ceremonies: Good evening. My name is _____,
and I'm pleased to serve as master of ceremonies as we honor
_____ for attaining Scouting's highest rank, the Eagle
Scout Award. This is a great moment worthy of celebration.

Tonight's court of honor will be a little different from those we are
accustomed to. Usually, the court of honor represents the culmination
of a young man's time in Scouting, and we are preparing to send him
out into the greater world to live the life of an Eagle. In our honoree's
case, however, he has already been living that life. *(Describes briefly*

how the honoree is living as an Eagle Scout, something like "As a student at Asbury College, he has participated in an overseas mission trip and been a leader in the faith life of his peers.") So tonight, we celebrate not just the end of a Scouting career, but the beginning of a life of service.

Before we begin our program, I'd like to introduce a few special people. *(Introduces key troop leaders, representatives of the chartered organization, presenters, and special guests.)*

I'd like to remind you all that there will be a reception honoring our new Eagle immediately following the ceremony. *(Other announcements, as necessary, are made here.)*

Now please rise for the invocation, presented by _____, and remain standing for the presentation of the colors and the Pledge of Allegiance.

Religious Leader or Chaplain Aide: *(Presents an invocation.)*

Scouts: *(Present the colors. One Scout leads the group in the Pledge of Allegiance.)*

Master of Ceremonies: By the power vested in me by the National Council of the Boy Scouts of America, I declare this court of honor to be duly convened for the sole purpose of presenting the Eagle Scout Award to _____.

Scouting Segment: Scout Law Candle Ceremony

(On a table at the front is a candelabrum with 12 candles, representing the points of the Scout Law, along with a 13th candle, representing the Spirit of Scouting. An older Scout, perhaps the senior patrol leader, stands behind the candles, holding the lighted "Spirit" candle.)

Master of Ceremonies: Robert Baden-Powell, the founder of Scouting, once said, "There is no religious side to the movement; the whole of it is based on religion, that is on the realization and service of God." In keeping with that spirit, let's consider how the Scout Law aligns with Scripture.

Scout: A Scout is trustworthy.

Master of Ceremonies: You shall not give false testimony against your neighbor – Exodus 20:16.

Scout: A Scout is loyal.

Master of Ceremonies: Whoever can be trusted with very little can also be trusted with much, and whoever is dishonest with very little will also be dishonest with much. – Luke 16:10

Scout: A Scout is helpful.

Master of Ceremonies: There will always be poor people in the land. Therefore I command you to be openhanded toward your fellow Israelites who are poor and needy in your land. – Deuteronomy 15:11

Scout: A Scout is friendly.

Master of Ceremonies: How good and pleasant it is when God's people live together in unity! – Psalm 133:1

Scout: A Scout is courteous.

Master of Ceremonies: Do not let any unwholesome talk come out of your mouths, but only what is helpful for building others up according to their needs, that it may benefit those who listen. – Ephesians 4:29

Scout: A Scout is kind.

Master of Ceremonies: The righteous care for the needs of their animals, but the kindest acts of the wicked are cruel. – Proverbs 12:10

Scout: A Scout is obedient.

Master of Ceremonies: Children, obey your parents in the Lord, for this is right. "Honor your father and mother" – which is the first commandment with a promise – "so that it may go well with you and that you may enjoy long life on the earth." – Ephesians 6:1-3

Scout: A Scout is cheerful.

Master of Ceremonies: A happy heart makes the face cheerful, but heartache crushes the spirit. – Proverbs 15:13

Scout: A Scout is thrifty.

Master of Ceremonies: Go to the ant, you sluggard; consider its ways and be wise! It has no commander, no overseer or ruler, yet it stores its provisions in summer and gathers its food at harvest. – Proverbs 6:6-8

Scout: A Scout is brave.

Master of Ceremonies: Be strong and courageous. Do not be afraid or terrified because of them, for the Lord your God goes with you; he will never leave you nor forsake you. – Deuteronomy 31:6

Scout: A Scout is clean.

Master of Ceremonies: Who may ascend the mountain of the Lord? Who may stand in his holy place? The one who has clean hands and a pure heart, who does not trust in an idol or swear by a false god. – Psalm 24:3-4

Scout: A Scout is reverent.

Master of Ceremonies: Love the Lord your God with all your heart and with all your soul and with all your mind and with all your strength. – Mark 12:30

(The Scout blows out the 13th candle and returns to his seat.)

Eagle Segment: The Eagle in History

Master of Ceremonies: I'd now like to ask _____ to come forward and discuss some of the symbolism inherent in the Eagle Scout Award.

Reader: The use of the eagle to represent Scouting's best is very appropriate. The eagle is, of course, our national bird, adorning our coins, several state flags, and the Great Seal of the United States of America.

But the symbolism of the eagle goes back much farther in time. In fact, the eagle has symbolized humankind's best since the dawn of recorded history.

The eagle has long been a symbol of good triumphing over evil. The ancient Greeks depicted the eagle holding a serpent in its claws, much as the American eagle holds arrows and an olive branch. So too the Eagle Scout battles evil in the world with the good in himself.

Armies from ancient Rome to nineteenth-century Europe have marched under eagle standards. Sioux warriors adorned their war bonnets with eagle feathers. Since 1912, an army of Eagle Scouts, more than two million strong, has gone out to build a better world for themselves and their fellow men.

Many cultures, watching the eagle fly toward the sun, have associated the bird with their sun gods. To the Assyrians, for example, the eagle represented the sun god Ashur; and in early Christianity, the eagle symbolized the ascension of Christ into heaven. Today the Eagle Scout continues to fly high, his gaze always fixed on his goals.

For countless centuries, the eagle has represented victory and valor, grace and beauty. The Eagle Scout represents those things, as well as the values embodied in the Scout Oath and Law.

The eagle is a rare creature. When you see one flying, you can't help but stop and watch its graceful, exuberant soaring. The Eagle Scout is a rare creature, too. Just watch him fly.

The Presentation of the Eagle Badge

Master of Ceremonies: It's now time for the highlight of our program: the presentation of the Eagle Scout Award. I'd like to ask Scoutmaster _____ to come forward to make the appropriate presentations.

(Note: If it's been a couple of years since the honoree earned his Eagle Scout Award, the current Scoutmaster may not be someone he worked with. In that case, consider using the former Scoutmaster instead.)

Scoutmaster: Would the honoree please come forward.

We have heard a lot tonight about what it means to be an Eagle Scout. Now our honoree will have the chance to tell us a little about what being an Eagle Scout means to him.

Honoree: *(Talks about what he's learned in the program, what the highlights of his time in Scouting have been, and what being an Eagle means to him. If the Scout wants to give the Scoutmaster or a mentor a gift, this would be an appropriate time.)*

Scoutmaster: As you've already learned, becoming an Eagle Scout is not the end of a journey; it is merely the beginning. So where do you go from here? _____ is here to tell you.

"Charger": As you stand here today, your time as a Scout is behind you. You've graduated from high school, have begun college, and are already thinking about where life will take you. So if I were to talk to you about merit badges and service projects, and living by the Scout Oath and Scout Law, you might well say, "Been there. Done that. Got the T-shirt."

But as someone who traveled the same path as you just a few decades ago, I have a little secret for you. The lessons you learned in Scouting will mean more – not less – in the years to come.

Let's start with merit badges. When you worked on merit badges, you explored topics you may have know nothing about at first. You had to learn the basics, master the skills, and perhaps most importantly motivate yourself to finish. Well, guess what? College classes are just like that. So are hobbies. And so will be your first job. People who are stuck in high school mode – who need teachers and parents to motivate them or who aren't interested in mastering new skills – rarely have exciting, fulfilling lives. Those who approach life as a series of merit badges live life to the fullest. I challenge you to approach life that way and to earn all the badges you can.

So what about service projects? The skills you learned in carrying out your Eagle project may help you handle major projects in college and career. More importantly, however, the satisfaction you felt in completing your project should spur you on to greater acts of service. Your country and your community need you to make a difference, to be a contributor to society, not just a consumer. I challenge you to make your Eagle project the first of many that you complete.

And finally, the Scout Oath and Law. As a child, you got your values from your parents, your church, and your school. I don't have to tell you that college is not like that, and that's why so many college students falter. As an old country song said, "You have to stand for something, or you'll fall for anything." In college – and in adulthood – your values have to come from within. You long ago memorized the words of the Oath and Law. I challenge you to live those words out, to use them as a compass that guides your thoughts and actions in the years to come.

So that's my challenge to you: learn all you can, serve all the time, and always live by the Scout Oath and Law.

Welcome to the brotherhood of Eagle Scouts.

Scoutmaster: Many times as a Scout, you joined with your fellow Scouts in repeating the Scout Oath. Now, you will stand alone and repeat a new oath, the Eagle Scout Promise. Though the words you say are similar to those you've said so many times before, tonight they will mean more to you than they ever have. When you pledge yourself on your sacred honor, you will be sealing your oath with the words that closed the Declaration of Independence.

I'd like all Eagle Scouts in the audience to stand at this time and rededicate themselves by repeating the Eagle Scout Promise with our new Eagle Scout.

Please make the Scout sign and repeat after me:

> I reaffirm my allegiance
> To the three promises of the Scout Oath.
> I thoughtfully recognize
> And take upon myself
> The obligations and responsibilities
> Of an Eagle Scout.
> On my honor I will do my best
> To make my training and example,
> My rank and my influence
> Count strongly for better Scouting
> And for better citizenship
> In my troop,
> In my community,
> And in my contacts with other people.
> To this I pledge my sacred honor.

Two. *(To Eagles in audience)* Please be seated.

Scoutmaster: Would the honor guard please escort the candidate's parents forward.

(Addressing the honoree) _____, your parents have undoubtedly been your primary source of help and strength.

No one will ever know the unnumbered acts of self-sacrifice from your mother. I'd like your mother to pin the Eagle medal on your uniform. *(She does so.)*

In recognition of your mother's devotion, please present her with this Eagle mother's pin. *(Scout pins on mother's pin.)*

Your father has been the source of much advice and guidance along the Eagle trail, so I'd like him to present the Eagle Scout certificate to you. *(He does so.)*

In return, please present your father with this Eagle lapel pin. *(He does so.)*

(Facing the audience) And now, it gives me great pleasure to present to you our newest Eagle Scout, _____!

(The audience responds with a standing ovation, which you may need to initiate.)

Scoutmaster: We're not through yet, however.

(At this time, any other presentations – from the troop, chartered organization, etc. – are made. The Scoutmaster may also read excerpts from congratulatory letters received. When he is finished, he congratulates the honoree and sits down.)

Closing Period

Master of Ceremonies: Tonight has indeed been a special night. Thank you all for coming out and participating in this wonderful event. Let's give our new Eagle Scout one more round of applause.

I now call on _____ to give our benediction.

Religious Leader or Chaplain Aide: *(Gives benediction.)*

Master of Ceremonies: Again, thank you for coming. Please join us at the reception. Good night.

Chapter 8

Support Functions

A discussion of the support functions necessary to a successful court of honor

Support Functions

The ceremony itself is only half of the court of honor. The other half
includes things like decorations, physical arrangements, and – perhaps
most importantly – food.

In this chapter are job descriptions for seven support volunteers, the
people who coordinate physical arrangements, publicity, decorations,
refreshments, the printed program, congratulatory letters, and photog-
raphy/videography. Sometimes, of course, one person may have to wear
several hats – in fact, you may end up doing all the jobs described here!
But I think it's important to work toward the ideal of having one person
do one job.

Many troops have developed traditions to ensure that the support
functions get taken care of. A member of the troop committee might
solicit congratulatory letters every time, for example. Or the families of
previous Eagle recipients might take care of decorations and refreshments for new honorees.

In addition to the seven job descriptions, this chapter includes sum-
maries of each job (starting on page 152) and a number of useful charts,
checklists, and samples.

continued on page 141

Facility Needs Worksheet

Photocopy this worksheet and use it to determine what sort of facility you'll need for the court of honor and reception. Also use it to record important information about the facility you decide to use.

Estimated attendance* _____

Facility Requirements

    Number of chairs _____   Number of tables _____
    Restrooms _____   Open stage _____
    Disabled access _____   Stage with curtain _____
    Kitchen _____   Reception area _____
    Other (specify) _____

Equipment Requirements

    Public-address system _____   Lectern _____
    Spotlights _____   Projection screen _____
    Other (specify) _____

Desired Dates and Times

    Rehearsal _____
    Set-up _____
    Court of honor _____

Facility Details

    Facility name _____
    Mailing address _____
    Location/directions _____
    Phone number _____
    Contact person _____
    Notes _____

* A room feels comfortably full when about 85 percent of the seats are taken, so aim for a room that's roughly 20 percent bigger than your estimated attendance.

Equipment and Awards Checklist

Even the simplest court of honor requires a lot of equipment. The following checklist should help you get started.

Equipment and Supplies	Assigned To
Public-address system	_____
Lectern	_____
PC and video projector	_____
CD player	_____
Projection screen	_____
TV and DVD player	_____
Candelabrums	_____
Candles	_____
Matches	_____
Flags (U.S., state, troop, patrol)	_____
Extension cords	_____
Three-pronged adapters	_____
Advancement board	_____
Lighted Eagle display	_____
Invitations	_____
Printed programs	_____

Awards and Recognition Items	Assigned To
Eagle badge	_____
Eagle pocket patch and/or square knot	_____
Mother's pin	_____
Father's lapel pin	_____
Mentor pins	_____
Eagle certificate (could be framed)	_____
Letter from Chief Scout Executive	_____
Other awards (belt buckle, plaque, ring, etc.)	_____
Congratulatory letters in scrapbook	_____
Flowers for mother	_____
NESA certificate (could be framed)	_____

Physical Arrangements Coordinator

Your responsibilities as physical-arrangements coordinator range from securing a location for the court of honor to providing matches to light the candles for the candle ceremony. You are critical to the success of the court of honor.

The first thing you should do is complete the facility needs worksheet on the page 139. By completing this form first, you will have a better idea of what sort of facility you need.

Secure a location as soon as possible. The court of honor can't really be promoted until you have a firm date and location. Confirm all arrangements in writing, and be sure you will have access to the building when you need it. Make sure you find an appropriate location, not only one that's the right size but one that has the right atmosphere. (See page 11 for ideas on picking a location.)

Your other big job is assembling all the equipment, props, and awards that are required. The checklist on the previous page will help you remember what you need.

On the day of the court of honor, you'll need to make sure the lights, public-address system, and electrical outlets work and that all props are in place. You'll also need to set the heater or air conditioner to a comfortable level. In general, especially in a crowded room, you should set the thermostat cooler than normal to allow for body heat to warm the room up. And be sure you have chairs in place on stage for the master of ceremonies and other presenters as needed.

Depending on your location, you may need to put up directional signs or post Scouts to help guests find their way. If guests have to travel a long way from the parking lot, create a virtual trail to Eagle for them to follow by mounting oversized rank badges along the route. (Start with the Boy Scout Insignia Card Set, available in the BSA catalog.)

Awards should be laid out on a table on stage or wherever the presentations will be made. Lay the awards out in the order they'll be used, and remove the pin backs from the Eagle badge and other awards. Be sure there's room for the honoree to set things he's given (like the Eagle Scout certificate) so he's able to shake hands or hug his parents.

Some troops lay the Eagle badge on a fancy pillow and carry it forward at the appropriate time. If your troop does this, you'll need to provide the pillow. (See page 179 for details.)

During the ceremony, you may be called upon to turn off or dim the lights, so you should find the light switches in advance (and make sure they work!).

Don't forget to recruit some people to help you set up and later clean up the building.

Publicity Coordinator

One of the most common mistakes in Eagle courts of honor is under-promotion, which leads to poor attendance. Sending plenty of invitations is one solution; the family should take care of this task.

The other solution is publicity. As publicity coordinator, your work can greatly increase attendance at the court of honor – and greatly increase public recognition of the boy's achievement.

The easy part of publicizing the court of honor is promoting it within the troop. Make sure the date is announced at troop meetings and in the troop newsletter. Also make sure that the patrol leaders call their Scouts a few days beforehand to remind them to attend.

Publicizing the court of honor outside the troop is a little harder, but still important.

Start by developing a list of newspapers, newsletters, and bulletins that might publicize the event. Your list should include local daily and weekly newspapers, the chartered organization's newsletter, the newsletter at the boy's place of worship, and newsletters published by the boy's parents' employers.

Next, gather information that can be used in a media release. This should include information about the boy and his family, the troop, and the ceremony itself. The worksheet on the next page covers what you need to know.

Creating a media release is pretty easy. Put the key details in the first few sentences and supporting information toward the end. Emphasize the significance of the Scout's achievement.

Write short, direct sentences, and use two- or three-sentence paragraphs. Be specific and factual. Make sure your story tells who, what, when, where, why, and how. It also helps to focus on what is unusual, interesting, or relevant to the reader.

continued on page 145

Media Release Worksheet

Before writing your media release, gather all the information you can about the Eagle Scout, the troop, and the court of honor itself. By completing this worksheet you'll have plenty of information to use in your media release. Remember to answer the questions who, what, when, where, why, and how.

Scout's name _____ Age _____
School and grade _____
Religious affiliation _____

Parents' names _____
Parents' employers _____

Scouting honors _____
Leadership positions held _____
Details of Eagle project _____
_____

Troop number _____
Scoutmaster _____
Chartered organization _____

Other activities (sports, band, etc.) _____
Other honors and positions _____

Court of honor date and time _____
Court of honor location _____
Description of ceremony _____
Key presenters _____

Other information (first Eagle in troop, major obstacles overcome, etc.)

_____
_____
_____
_____
_____

Sample Media Release

Once you've completed the media release worksheet on page 143, compose a release similar to the one below. Remember to write short, direct sentences and put key information near the top. Your release should be formatted like the sample.

FOR IMMEDIATE RELEASE   CONTACT: PAUL JONES

555-1212

LOCAL BOY TO RECEIVE EAGLE SCOUT AWARD

Since he was nine years old, Jonathan Springer has had just two wishes — to become an Eagle Scout and to become a newspaper editor like his father, Bob. On Wednesday, Feb. 8, he'll get his first wish.

Jonathan, 18, of Boy Scout Troop 317, will be honored at a special Eagle Scout ceremony at 7 p.m. at Christ Church United Methodist. The public is invited to attend.

To earn Scouting's highest award, Jonathan had to earn 21 merit badges, serve as a leader in his troop, and complete a major community service project.

Jonathan's service project took place in the Daniel Boone National Forest. Leading 19 Scouts and adults, Jonathan built an outdoor classroom and a two-mile nature trail at the Piney Woods Campground. The project took more than two months to complete.

Jonathan has been a member of Troop 317, chartered to Christ Church United Methodist, for 6 years. He has served the troop as patrol leader, quartermaster, instructor, and senior patrol leader. He has also worked at Camp Tall Pines for the past three summers.

Jonathan is a senior at Central High School. He plans to enter the journalism program at the University of Mississippi next fall.

—END—

The sample release on page 144 will get you started. As you can see, it is double-spaced, has a contact name and phone number, says "For immediate release" at the beginning, and says "End" at the end. Your release should do the same.

Once your release is complete, mail or email it to everyone on your list. Send it a week before the event to daily newspapers, two weeks before to weekly publications, and as early as possible to monthly publications. If possible, send a portrait shot of the honoree with each release. When sending a print, write the Scout's name on the back with a felt-tip pen, then paper-clip the photo to the release.

Follow up with phone calls. Make sure the publication received your release and ask that they print it. With newspapers, talk to the assignments editor or features editor. Many newspapers have a standard procedure for Eagle announcements (along with announcements of events such as graduations); find out what that procedure is and follow it.

I recommend sending a second release after the court of honor. This can be the same thing you sent before; just change the verbs to past tense.

Decorations Coordinator

Your job is relatively easy but still important. The way the room is decorated helps establish the mood for the ceremony.

One thing you'll probably want is a backdrop behind the stage or presentation area. A Scouting wall drape or banner makes a good backdrop and can probably be borrowed from your council service center. Another idea is to project a photo of the Eagle badge or of the honoree onto the wall with a video projector.

I also recommend setting up a table to display some of the honoree's Scouting memorabilia, including his Cub Scout uniform, patch vest, scrapbooks, etc. A display like this is fun to look at and helps to personalize the court of honor. See "Decorating Ideas" on page 146 for more possibilities.

You'll probably want to work closely with the refreshments coordinator on table decorations. One idea is to anchor helium balloons inside old Boy Scout popcorn tins filled with crumpled paper. If the court of honor falls near Independence Day, you should have no trouble finding balloons, bunting, tablecloths, centerpieces, and an infinite array of other patriotic decorating items.

Refreshments Coordinator

Eagle courts of honor traditionally end with a reception, which usually centers around food. As refreshments coordinator, your job is to buy and/ or make that food and serve it. You'll also need to take care of things like plates, utensils, punch bowls, and napkins.

The most common food item is a sheet cake, although cupcakes let you avoid the ceremonial cutting of the cake, which can slow the reception down if the honoree is still shaking hands. If you do go with a sheet cake, visit **cakes.com** to find a local bakery that has licensed BSA logos or ask your favorite bakery if it can transfer a photo of the honoree onto the cake. (A photo of him as a Tenderfoot Scout can be especially fun.)

Be sure to buy the right size cake for the crowd you expect. Bakeries typically describe three portion sizes: dessert size (2" x 4"), receiving-line size (2" x 3"), and buffet size (2" x 2"). For a full sheet cake (16" x 24") those numbers translate into 48, 64, and 96 servings, respectively. Half a sheet cake (12" x 16") would, of course, yield half as many servings.

Decorating Ideas

Here are some things you can use to decorate for the court of honor. Can you think of other things to use?

The honoree's memorabilia (patch vest, scrapbooks, Cub Scout uniform, etc.)
Tablecloths
Centerpieces
Red, white, and blue crepe-paper streamers
Red, white, and blue balloons
Boy Scout insignia posters
American flag
Troop and patrol flags
Advancement board

Eagle Scout banner
BSA banner
Scout emblem for lectern
Stage backdrop
Norman Rockwell or Joseph Csatari prints, mounted on mat board
Photo albums
Model campsite
A giant congratulations card, signed by all the members of the troop

Other items could include punch, mixed nuts, cookies, ice cream, or whatever you and the family prefer. Wedding-planning websites are a great source for ideas, from monogrammed M&Ms to candy bars with custom-printed wrappers.

Don't overdo it, though. After all, the reception is just the icing on the cake, so to speak.

A suggested shopping list appears below.

Printed Program Coordinator

The printed program serves as the agenda for the court of honor and as a souvenir for people to take home.

You can buy several styles of Eagle program covers from your local Scout Shop or you can design your own.

Most program covers are either 8½" x 11" (letter size) or 5½" x 8½" (half letter size). The larger size obviously gives you more space to work with, but you can add additional sheets to either size if you need to. A classy way to bind multisheet programs is by tying the sheets together with thin gold cord.

Whatever program covers you choose, you can have the programs printed professionally or photocopy them yourself. If you go the professional route, it's cheaper to provide camera-ready copy. You may also need

---

Reception Shopping List

Here's what you'll need for a cake-and-punch reception. Don't assume that the facility you're using will have any of these things unless you check first.

Cake	Cream	Knife for cake
Ice cream	Cups (punch and coffee)	Punch bowl
Cookies	Plates	Ladle
Punch	Napkins	Coffee pot
Coffee	Utensils	Extension cord
Sugar and sweetener	Serving utensils	Clean-up supplies

to allow a week or more for printing.

The only thing the program really has to include is the ceremony agenda; this outline is usually found inside the program on the right side. (See the sample below.)

Other items you can include are a profile of the honoree, a summary of his Scouting career, his photo, family information, a personal message from him, information about the Eagle Scout Award itself, an Eagle Scout poem, or a list of past Eagle Scouts from the troop (including the years they received their Eagle badges).

Keep in mind that some guests won't be familiar with Scouting. The program gives you an opportunity to educate them.

Boy Scout Troop 317

Eagle Scout Court of Honor
In Recognition of Jonathan Springer
February 8, 2012

Call to Order	*Paul Jones* *Asst. Scoutmaster*
Invocation	*Rev. Joseph Grayson* *Christ Church UM*
Opening Ceremony	*Eagle Patrol*
The Scout Law	*Viking Patrol*
"Eagle Mountain"	*Kevin Whitley* *Eagle Scout*
Presentation of the *Eagle Badge*	*Henry J. Wright* *Scoutmaster*
Closing	*Paul Jones*

Please join us after the ceremony for a reception
in honor of our newest Eagle.

Sample Program

As this sample shows, the printed program doesn't have to be fancy or expensive to be effective. See page 147 for other items to include in the program.

Congratulatory Letter Coordinator

One popular court-of-honor tradition is to have someone read aloud excerpts from congratulatory letters the honoree has received. The reading often starts with a letter from the mayor and culminates with a letter from the President of the United States; interspersed might be letters from religious leaders, sports heroes, movie stars, or other famous people.

Many public figures have standard letters that they're happy to send out to new Eagle Scouts; others will send proclamations or certificates. As the congratulatory letter coordinator, your job is to solicit these letters and mementos, which means you have to compile a list, find addresses, prepare letters, and send them out in time for the court of honor. To make this task a little easier, *The Eagle Court of Honor Book* website (**www .eaglebook.com**) includes links to several dignitary lists that Scouters have compiled and posted online. (Some lists also note those people who have requested not to be contacted.)

Like everything else about the court of honor, however, you should customize the list for the honoree. If he's a lifelong Presbyterian who cares little for sports, don't request letters from the local Catholic arch-bishop or the coach of the Dallas Cowboys. Instead, seek out people who are meaningful in his life. And don't leave out people who may be celebrities only in the new Eagle's eyes, such as an out-of-town grandparent who can't attend the court of honor. These personal letters are more meaningful than the canned responses celebrities send.

There are a few pointers you should keep in mind when requesting letters. First, you'll probably get better results if you explicitly ask for a congratulatory letter instead of just sending an invitation. (This may also reduce the number of letters that begin with "I'm sorry that my schedule does not permit me to be with you on this special occasion.") See the sample letter on the next page. Second, consider enclosing a self-addressed stamped envelope, especially when writing to people who likely can't afford to send out hundreds of letters a year. Finally, send your requests as soon as possible after the board of review to ensure that the letters arrive in time for the court of honor.

When the letters arrive, make photocopies of them and put the originals in a binder or scrapbook. (If they come in various sizes, an expanding

continued on page 151

Sample Congratulatory Letter Request

Use a request like this to solicit congratulatory letters. Your request should tell something about the new Eagle and explain exactly what you'd like the recipient to do: send a congratulatory letter to you by the date specified.

Dear Congressman Smith:

On February 8, 2012, Boy Scout Jonathan Springer, a member of Troop 317 in Louisville, will be honored at a special court of honor for achieving the Eagle Scout Award, Boy Scouting's highest honor. In your position, I know you recognize the importance of this achievement in this young man's life.

To become an Eagle Scout, Jonathan earned 21 merit badges and served his troop in a variety of leadership roles. He also completed a major community service project, building an outdoor classroom and a two-mile nature trail at the Piney Woods Campground in the Daniel Boone National Forest. A senior at Central High School, he plans to enter the University of Mississippi next fall, where he will study journalism.

To make the ceremony even more special, we are compiling letters of congratulations from people like you. Would you please consider sending along such a letter, plus any other items you wish to have presented to him? Please send your items to the above address by January 31. We will put the letters we receive in a scrapbook and present them at the ceremony.

Thank you so much for taking the time to help us honor this special young man.

Sincerely,

Paul Jones
Assistant Scoutmaster

cardstock wallet from an office-supply store is a good option.) Then, go through the photocopies and highlight those sections that you want to read at the court of honor. A little careful editing can greatly increase the impact of reading the letters.

Photography/Videography Coordinator

Perhaps the biggest regret parents have after an Eagle court of honor is that nobody recorded the moment for posterity. There's no video of the presentation of the Eagle badge, no recording of the moving charge the Scoutmaster gave, nothing but fading memories to preserve the moment.

As photography/videography coordinator, you can help prevent those regrets. Your job, simply put, is to record the event by either taking photos and videos yourself or by coordinating the work of other photographers and videographers.

To be effective, you and other photographers and videographers shouldn't have any other role in the event that would distract you from shooting (including mingling with guests at the reception). You should also review the script ahead of time and be aware of specific moments than need to be captured: pinning the Eagle badge, making the speech, cutting the cake, etc. Be sure you know how lighting and room arrangements will affect your work.

One photo you should definitely take is a portrait of the honoree in uniform, either on the day of the ceremony or a few days before. Before works especially well because the photo can then be used in the printed program or onscreen as a backdrop.

If you're coordinating the photography/videography and not doing the work yourself, check with local high schools or colleges that have audiovisual departments. You may well find a talented student who can do a professional-quality job at a starving-artist price.

After the ceremony, give the family and the troop CDs or DVDs containing all the photos and video you shot.

Support Job Summaries

Physical Arrangements Coordinator

—Determine what sort of location you need. (See facility needs worksheet on page 139.)
—Arrange to use the building. Complete any necessary rental agreements or other forms.
—Arrange access for rehearsal, set-up, and the court of honor itself.
—Confirm all details in writing.
—Visit the building to check facilities.
—Recruit volunteers to set up the room before the court of honor.
—Recruit volunteers to clean up the room after the court of honor.
—Arrange for all needed equipment and supplies. (See equipment checklist on page 140.)
—Confirm access the day before the court of honor.
—Recheck the public-address system, lights, outlets, etc.
—Make sure the heater or air conditioner is properly set.
—Reserve seats for the honoree and his family, presenters, and special guests.
—Supervise set-up.
—Supervise clean-up.

Publicity Coordinator

—Develop a target list for media releases.
—Gather adequate information to create a media release. (Use the media release worksheet on page 143.)
—Prepare a media release. (See the example on page 144.)
—Mail or email copies to the media before the court of honor.
—Follow up media releases by phone.
—Promote the court of honor within the troop.
—Prepare a second media release after the court of honor.
—Mail copies to the media after the court of honor.

Decorations Coordinator

—Buy or borrow decorations as needed. (See list of suggested decorating supplies on page 146.)
—Encourage the honoree to bring patch vest, scrapbooks, and other items.
—Arrange for the room to be decorated before the court of honor.
—Arrange for decorations to be taken down and returned to their owners after the court of honor.
—Work within the budget set by the court of honor coordinator.

Refreshments Coordinator

—Order and/or make the cake and other refreshments. (See the shopping list on page 147.)
—Arrange for plates, cups, utensils, etc.
—Recruit servers.
—Arrange for clean-up of the reception area and kitchen.
—Work within the budget set by the court of honor coordinator.

Printed Program Coordinator

—Buy or create program covers.
—Get the ceremony agenda from the court of honor coordinator.
—Get other materials as needed, such as a list of the Scout's achievements or a photo.
—Have the program typed or typeset. (See the example on page 148.)
—Have the programs printed.
—Pick up the programs from the printer and take them to the ceremony.
—Recruit Scouts to distribute the programs at the ceremony.
—Work within the budget set by the court of honor coordinator.

Congratulatory Letter Coordinator

—Develop a mailing list of government and religious leaders, sports heroes, movie stars, and other famous people, as well as individuals who have been important in the Scout's growth and development.
—Write to these people and ask them to supply a congratulatory letter, certificate, or other recognition item. (See the sample request letter on page 150.)
—Make copies of the items received and highlight sections to be read at the court of honor.
—Put the originals in a binder or scrapbook to present to the honoree.
—Read excerpts of the letters at the court of honor.
—Work within the budget set by the court of honor coordinator.

Photography/Videography Coordinator

—Shoot video and/or photos of the entire event, from set-up through clean-up.
—Review the script and perhaps attend the rehearsal to develop a shooting plan.
—Take a formal portrait of the honoree in uniform, along with photos of him and his Scoutmaster, him and his parents, etc.
—Give copies of everything you shoot to the troop and the family after the court of honor.

Appendices

A. Charges

Becoming an Eagle Scout is a great accomplishment; being an Eagle Scout is a great responsibility. As an Eagle, the Scout Oath and Scout Law should take on new meaning for you; the motto and slogan take on new urgency.

As an Eagle, your first obligation is to live with honor. You are a marked man, a leader; for good or ill, people will follow the example you set. Give up anything before you give up your reputation and good name. As Shakespeare said, "Mine honor is my life; both grow in one. Take honor from me, and my life is done." Let the white of the Eagle badge remind you of honor.

Your second obligation as an Eagle Scout is to be loyal. As a follower, you promised to be loyal to those above you. Now, as a leader, you must also be loyal to those below you, treating them as you would want to be treated. And you must also be loyal to your ideals, not letting others sway you from your course. Let the blue of the Eagle badge remind you of loyalty.

Your third obligation as an Eagle Scout is to be courageous. Stepping into your new role as a leader, you will face many challenges and obstacles. A ship in the harbor is safe, but that's not what ships are for. You must have the courage to do what is right, no matter what other people do or say. Let the red of the Eagle badge remind you of courage.

Your fourth obligation is to serve others, for a leader is above all a servant. Let the practice of the daily good turn lead to a lifetime of service, for only in giving of yourself do you give anything of value. Just as it always has, let the scroll on your badge remind you of service.

Your final obligation as an Eagle Scout is to have vision. As a leader, you must now blaze your own trail. Just as a bald eagle soaring high above the ground can look far into the distance, so too must you look far into the future. Many people will follow you; only with vision will you lead them in the right direction. Let the silver eagle hanging from your badge remind you of vision.

These then are your obligations as an Eagle Scout: honor, loyalty, courage, service, and vision. By meeting these obligations, you can lead your troop, your community, your nation toward a better tomorrow.

We are here tonight, of course, to celebrate a great success. Now it is my job to tell you how to turn that success into more successes throughout the rest of your life.

So how can you be successful? What's the secret? It's simple: be a failure.

That may seem like strange advice, but when you think about it, you've been failing ever since you became a Scout.

Do you remember the first time you tried to build a fire? You failed, didn't you? And what about your first hike, the one that ended in sore muscles and blisters? You didn't win the first time you ran for patrol leader, and when you did win, you made plenty of mistakes when you tried to lead your patrol.

You're not the only who has failed. Thomas Edison discovered 1,800 ways not to make a light bulb before he invented one that worked. Babe Ruth struck out 1,330 times on his way to hitting a record-setting 714 home runs. Michael Jordan was cut from his high-school basketball team. Abraham Lincoln dropped out of school, lost two elections for the House of Representatives, and lost two elections for the Senate before becoming President.

But these men never let their failures get them down. Instead, they learned from their mistakes, improved themselves, and went on to enjoy great success.

So don't be afraid to make mistakes; don't be afraid to fail. Remember, if you've tried to do something and failed, you're vastly better off than if you'd tried to do nothing and succeeded.

As a representative of the Eagle Scouts of this council, I wish to welcome you to the brotherhood of Eagle Scouts. Only five percent of the boys who enter Scouting achieve what you have here tonight. The requirements are demanding but fair. Your achievement is recognition of your perseverance and ability.

But I am not here to talk of your past accomplishments, which are great, but of your future opportunities. _____ years ago, I received my Eagle award, and in the years since then, it has constantly enriched my life. It will yours. Of course, when you go to a Scouting function, you will be recognized as a doer, and you will have the opportunity of standing as a leader among leaders.

But I think that your Eagle award will have meaning far beyond Scouting itself. You are a marked man, and your achievement will follow you throughout your life. The things you have done, the leadership and sense of honor you have developed will mean more to you than a certificate and a piece of ribbon. You will have more opportunity to be of service to your fellow man through your school, your work, and through Scouting, because you know what you can do.

In the years to come, you will casually meet people who are Eagles too, and there will be an instant bond of comradeship. You have each shared a common experience; you each know that the other can be trusted. The comradeship among Eagles extends throughout the world of Scouting and into the larger world beyond. For the rest of your life, you travel as a marked man, an Eagle Scout. Welcome!

During your time in Scouting, you have learned and lived the Cub Scout Promise, the Law of the Pack, the Cub Scout motto, [the Venturing Oath and Code,] and of course the Scout Oath, Law, motto, and slogan.

Each time you were presented with a new code of conduct, the words were unfamiliar, and you struggled to memorize them. Later, of course, you could recite them as easily as you repeat your own name. They – and the lessons they taught – became a part of you.

Tonight, for the first time, you will repeat the Eagle Scout Promise. Again, some of the words will be unfamiliar, but as you live out the life of an Eagle, they too will become a part of you.

Making that new promise does not mean that you should forget all the other promises. Instead, I challenge you to always remember and live by all the promises you've made as a Scout, all the codes you've agreed to follow. By doing that, you will prove yourself worthy of the Eagle badge you receive tonight.

Congratulations! You've made it. You've climbed the Eagle mountain. I applaud your achievement.

But now it's time to look toward the future, toward those others mountains out on the horizon.

How are you going to climb them? The same way you climbed the Eagle mountain. Just remember the things you learned on your way to Eagle, and you'll be able to climb any mountain, to overcome any obstacle.

Do you remember when you first looked up at the Eagle mountain? How high it seemed back then. But you took that first step along the trail and began climbing. One step at a time, you followed the trail blazed by others. Then, when that path faded away, you blazed your own trail, a trail that others are now following.

And finally, always keeping your eye on the goal, you reached the top.

You have many mountains waiting to be climbed. Some may seem insurmountable, but they can all be conquered. Just set your goal, take that first step, follow the blazed trail until it's time to blaze your own, and always keep your eye on the goal.

Good luck and good climbing!

A favorite Scripture verse for many people who work with young people is 1 Timothy 4:12, which begins "Don't let anyone put you down because you're young." We hold tightly to that verse because we recognize that many adults – even some in the church – do look down on young people precisely because they are young. These adults may complain about loud music and fast cars and declining moral standards, but the bottom line is that they can't imagine today's young people becoming tomorrow's leaders. And they've forgotten their own younger days.

So we repeat those words like an incantation: "Don't let anyone put you down because you're young." "Don't let anyone put you down because you're young." "Don't let anyone put you down because you're young."

But we sometimes leave out the rest of the verse. In *The Message*, Eugene Peterson's translation of the Bible, that second half goes like this: "Teach believers with your life: by word, by demeanor, by love, by faith, by integrity."

In other words, it's not enough to just stand up for yourself. You also have to stand for something.

Not surprisingly, the obligations of an Eagle Scout – honor, loyalty, courage, service, and vision – echo those listed in 1 Timothy. In a few minutes, you'll pledge yourself – on your sacred honor – to fulfill the obligations and responsibilities of an Eagle Scout.

But here's your challenge – and your opportunity. While there are detailed requirements for becoming an Eagle Scout, there are no requirements at all for being an Eagle Scout. The path you've been climbing since you joined Scouting ends right now. Right on this stage. The path you follow from here on out is yours to blaze.

You may embark on a lifetime of service to Scouting, giving back to the program that's given you so much, but you may never put on a Scout uniform again. You may choose a rewarding career, one that brings you fame and fortune, but you make take any old job so you can spend more time with your family. You may strive to make the world a better place by pursuing a career in teaching or community service, but you may decide you can better serve in other ways.

And guess what. It doesn't really matter. Wherever you go, you'll go as an Eagle Scout. Whatever you do, the values the badge represents will guide your steps.

So my challenge to you is simple: "Teach with your life: by word, by demeanor, by love, by faith, by integrity."

Congratulations!

As you stand here today, your time as a Scout is behind you. You've graduated from high school, have begun college, and are already thinking about where life will take you. So if I were to talk to you about merit badges and service projects, and living by the Scout Oath and Scout Law, you might well say, "Been there. Done that. Got the T-shirt."

But as someone who traveled the same path as you just a few decades ago, I have a little secret for you. The lessons you learned in Scouting will mean more – not less – in the years to come.

Let's start with merit badges. When you worked on merit badges, you explored topics you may have know nothing about at first. You had to learn the basics, master the skills, and perhaps most importantly motivate yourself to finish. Well, guess what? College classes are just like that. So are hobbies. And so will be your first job. People who are stuck in high school mode – who need teachers and parents to motivate them or who aren't interested in mastering new skills – rarely have exciting, fulfilling lives. Those who approach life as a series of merit badges live life to the fullest. I challenge you to approach life that way and to earn all the badges you can.

So what about service projects? The skills you learned in carrying out your Eagle project may help you handle major projects in college and career. More importantly, however, the satisfaction you felt in completing your project should spur you on to greater acts of service. Your country and your community need you to make a difference, to be a contributor to society, not just a consumer. I challenge you to make your Eagle project the first of many that you complete.

And finally, the Scout Oath and Law. As a child, you got your values from your parents, your church, and your school. I don't have to tell you that college is not like that, and that's why so many college students falter. As an old country song said, "You have to stand for something, or you'll fall for anything." In college – and in adulthood – your values have to come from within. You long ago memorized the words of the Oath and Law. I challenge you to live those words out, to use them as a compass that guides your thoughts and actions in the years to come.

So that's my challenge to you: learn all you can, serve all the time, and always live by the Scout Oath and Law.

Welcome to the brotherhood of Eagle Scouts.

B. Poems

The Eagle Scout
by S. Kurtz Hingley

A fond mother watches her boy where he stands,
    Apart from his comrades tonight
As they place on his camp-battered tunic a badge,
    An Eagle, the emblem of Right.

It seems to her just a few short months have passed
    Since he joined with the youngster next door.
How proud he was then of his Tenderfoot pin
    As he told her the message it bore.

But three years have gone as he struggled along,
    To learn what the Scout Law's about,
And he practiced them daily, that Oath and that Law,
    Until now – he's an Eagle Scout.

You may smile with your worldly wise wisdom at this,
    And say, "Why, it's only a pin."
But I tell you no honors he'll gain as a man
    Will mean just as much to him.

The red, white, and blue of the ribbon you see,
    Are symbols of honor and truth.
He has learned how to value these fine attributes
    In the glorious days of youth.

And the out-flinging wings of the Eagle that rests
     On the breast of this knight of today
Are the things which shall lift him above petty deeds,
     And guide him along the right way.

Yes, it's only a pin, just an Eagle Scout Badge,
     But the heart that's beneath it is true,
And will throb to the last for the things which are good
     A lesson for me – and for you.

The Eagle Scout

The Scouts gave you a challenge, and
You've met it faithfully, my friend,
But it's quite hard to understand
Just all it will mean in the end.

An Eagle Scout, you've reached the top,
Or have you only just begun?
I'm betting that you will not stop
With so much glory to be won.

For life holds out a challenge too,
A mountain high for you to scale,
And with the training Scouts gave you,
There's really no such word as "fail."

And so as you press on ahead,
You'll find it's made much work like play,
And as the tasks before you spread,
They'll find you ready, so I'll say.

Congratulations, Eagle Scout,
The world before you now is spread.
Scouts taught you much what life's about,
Prepared you well for what's ahead.

Voice of the Eagle

I am the Eagle.
I am prepared
To stand for virtues
Of freedom
      Strength
      And pride.

I am the Eagle.
I am prepared
To serve
      My God
      My country
      And other people.

I am the Eagle.
I am prepared
To stand for
      Honesty
      Truth
      And integrity.

I am the Eagle.
I am prepared
To lead others
      To accomplish set tasks
      To the best of my ability.

I am the Eagle.
I am prepared
To defend
      What makes America
great
      For all people.

I am the Eagle.
I am prepared
To cross all lines
      Of race, creed,
      And nationality.

I am the Eagle.
I am prepared
To be self-reliant
      And resourceful.

I am the Eagle.
I am prepared.

The Oyster and the Eagle

When God made the oyster, he guaranteed him social security.
He built the oyster a house ... a shell to protect him from his enemies.
When hungry, the oyster simply opens his shell and the food rushes in.
But when God made the eagle, He said, "The blue sky is the limit. Go
    and build your own house."

And the eagle went and built his house upon the highest mountain peak,
    where storms threaten him every day.
For food, he must fly through miles of rain and snow and wind.
The eagle then – not the oyster – is the symbol of the United States of
    America, and of Scouting's highest award.

The Eagle Scout Trail
by G.S. Ripley

The Eagle Scout, whose notable achievement
We honor here tonight, has just completed
A long, long trail. He started months ago
As Tenderfoot, the gateway to the trail,
With Scout Good Turns and slogan, "Be Prepared."
Then Second Class and First, with outdoor life,
The open road with nights beneath the stars,
And service to community and troop.
Now pinnacles of Star and Life were scaled,
On one hand learning skills and pioneering,
While following the daily Scout ideals
Of service in the home, the church, the school –
Not merely winning many merit badges,
But living out the Scout Oath and Law.

And yet the Eagle Scout who stands before us
Has not attained the summit. No, instead,
He's really just embarking on another trail
Much greater – that of Scouting leadership,
And, with the spirit of a true American,
Is ready to defend our way of life.

An Eagle Scout's Prayer

Now that I'm an Eagle Scout
And look back down the trail I've trod,
I can see what Scouting's all about,
And I offer this humble prayer to God.

I know now the Eagle badge isn't the end;
Its silver rays light a new height to ascend.
I know I could never have gotten this far
Without help from others who served as my stars.

So thank you, Lord, for my chance to be
A patriot proud in the land of the free.
Thank you for home and churches and schools.
Thank you for parents and teachers and rules.

Thank you for leaders who understand,
Who always stand ready to give me their hand.
Let me share with all people my gifts as they grow,
For I must try to repay the great debt that I owe.

Let me treat everyone as my sister or brother
And reward each good turn by doing another.
Make me fight the good battles though weary and scared.
Let me meet every crisis by being prepared.

Give me the wisdom and honor and courage to do
The things that are always pleasing to you.
Remind me if ever I start to stray
That other Eagles in khaki have paved my way.

Their ghosts are watching and waiting to see
That I live up to all that's expected of me.
If I should falter and fall toward the ground,
Stretch forth your arm so I won't let them down.

Write your purpose upon my willing heart
With a finger that's tipped in fire.
I have already gotten a good head start;
Help me to climb even higher.

I promise to strive for a worthy goal
That I know to be solid and right.
Lift up my wings and nourish my soul
As I dare the Eagle's flight.

Chart me a course that's straight and true
With the Scout Oath and Law as my guide.
Teach my body and mind and heart what to do,
So you can smile down on me with pride.

Keep me sharp as the edge of a whittling knife
To cut through the darkness and doubt.
Let me never forget as I soar through life
That I am an Eagle Scout.

Amen.

C. Quotations

Honor

Honor lies in honest toil.

Grover Cleveland

Better to die ten thousand deaths than wound my honor.

Joseph Addison

When faith is lost, when honor dies, the man is dead!

John Greenleaf Whittier

Mine honor is my life; both grow in one; take honor from me, and my life is done.

William Shakespeare

A good name is more desirable than great riches; to be esteemed is better than silver or gold.

Bible, Proverbs 22:1

Loyalty

Loyalty means nothing unless it has as its heart the absolute principle of self-sacrifice.

Anonymous

My country right or wrong; when right, to keep her right; when wrong, to put her right.

Carl Schurz

Unless you can find some sort of loyalty, you cannot find unity and peace in your active living.

Josiah Royce

This above all: to thine ownself be true,
And it must follow, as the night the day,
Thou canst not then be false to any man.

William Shakespeare

Courage

One man with courage makes a majority.

Andrew Jackson

Never run away from anything. Never!

Winston Churchill

Courage is resistance to fear, mastery of fear – not absence of fear.

Mark Twain

Last, but by no means least, courage – moral courage, the courage of one's convictions, the courage to see things through. The world is in a constant conspiracy against the brave. It's the age-old struggle – the roar of the crowd on one side and the voice of your conscience on the other.

Douglas MacArthur

I love the man that can smile in trouble, that can gather strength from distress, and grow brave by reflection. 'Tis the business of little minds to shrink; but he whose heart is firm, and whose conscience approves his conduct, will pursue his principles unto death.

Thomas Paine

The greatest test of courage on earth is to bear defeat without losing heart.

Robert Green Ingersoll

This is no time for ease and comfort. It is the time to dare and endure.

Winston Churchill

True courage is like a kite; a contrary wind raises it higher.

John Petit-Senn

Courage is grace under pressure.

Ernest Hemingway

A ship in harbour is safe, but that is not what ships are built for.

William Shedd

Service

The men and women who have the right ideals ... are those who have the courage to strive for the happiness which comes only with labor and effort and self-sacrifice, and those whose joy in life springs in part from power of work and sense of duty.

Theodore Roosevelt

It is one of the most beautiful compensations of this life that no man can sincerely try to help another without helping himself.

Ralph Waldo Emerson

The princes among us are those who forget themselves and serve mankind.

Woodrow Wilson

The more he cast away, the more he had.

John Bunyan

If there be any truer measure of a man than by what he does, it must be by what he gives.

Robert South

Far and away the best prize that life offers is the chance to work hard at work worth doing.

Theodore Roosevelt

Vision

Where there is no vision, the people perish.

Bible, Proverbs 29:18a

Only he who keeps his eye fixed on the far horizon will find his right road.

Dag Hammarskjöld

The farther back you can look, the farther forward you are likely to see.

Winston Churchill

Cherish your illusions and your dreams as they are the children of your soul – the blueprints of your ultimate achievements.

Napoleon Hill

People with goals succeed because they know where they're going.

Earl Nightingale

Far away, there in the sunshine, are my highest aspirations. I may not reach them, but I can look up and see their beauty, believe in them and try to follow where they lead.

Louisa May Alcott

Live your life each day as you would climb a mountain. An occasional glance toward the summit keeps the goal in mind, but many beautiful scenes are to be observed from each new vantage point. Climb slowly, steadily, enjoying each passing moment, and the view will serve as a fitting climax for the journey.

Harold V. Melchert

Obstacles are those frightful things you see when you take your eyes off your goals.

Anonymous

Shoot for the stars. So what if you only reach the moon!

Anonymous

The future belongs to those who believe in the beauty of their dreams.

Eleanor Roosevelt

Leadership

Blessed is the person who sees the need, recognizes the responsibility, and actively becomes the answer.

William Arthur Ward

Watch your step. Whether we will it or not, we cannot journey without leaving footprints, and others will follow where we go because we have marked the way.

Anonymous

Those who seek to lead should not cease to learn.

Anonymous

The good leader controls his team as a conductor inspires his orchestra. He weighs the difficulties ahead. He is a master of his craft. He knows the strong points and weaknesses of his musicians and of himself. He is willing to stand out in front and to lead from start to finish, through easy passages and through difficulties. At times he may give the soloist his head, but the soloist has his entry and exit; the conductor must be in charge right to the end.

Adam Arnold Brown

If he is indeed wise, he does not bid you enter the house of his wisdom, but rather leads you to the threshold of your own mind....

Kahlil Gibran

Leadership is action, not position.

D. H. McGannon

A leader is best when people barely know he exists,
Not so good when people obey and acclaim him
Worse when they despise him.
Fail to honor people,
They fail to honor you.
But of a good leader who talks little,
When his work is done, his aim fulfilled,
The people will say, "We did this ourselves."

Lao Tzu

People may doubt what you say, but they'll always believe what you do.

Anonymous

Do not follow where the path may lead. Go instead where there is no path and leave a trail.

Anonymous

Excellence

If a man is called to be a street sweeper, he should sweep streets even as Michelangelo painted, or Beethoven composed music, or Shakespeare wrote poetry. He should sweep streets so well that all the hosts of heaven and earth will pause to say, here lived a great street sweeper who did his job well.

Martin Luther King Jr.

Whatever you are, be a good one.

Abraham Lincoln

The only limit to our realization of tomorrow will be our doubts of today.

Franklin Delano Roosevelt

Use the talents you possess, for the woods would be very silent if no birds sang except the best.

Anonymous

It's your attitude and not your aptitude that determines your altitude.

Zig Ziglar

The difference between a successful person and others is not a lack of strength, not a lack of knowledge, but rather a lack of will.

Vince Lombardi

Excellence can be attained if you care more than others think is wise, risk more than others think is safe, dream more than others think is practical, and expect more than others think is possible.

Anonymous

Youth Development

It takes a whole community to raise a child.

African proverb

Train up a child in the way he should go; and when he is old, he will not depart from it.

Bible, Proverbs 22:6

Our ultimate object is to breed manly men for our respective countries, strong in body, mind and spirit; men who can be trusted; men who can face hard work and also hard times; men who can make up their own minds and not be led by mass suggestion; men who can sacrifice much that is personal in the greater good of the nation.

Lord Robert Baden-Powell

It isn't what the boy does to the board that counts – it's what the board does to the boy.

Handicraft: Pow Wow Section

There is always one moment in childhood when the door opens and lets the future in.

Graham Greene

Of all the animals, the boy is the most unmanageable.

Plato

You are the bows from which your children are as living arrows sent forth.

Kahlil Gibran

He that will have his son have respect for him and his orders must himself have a great reverence for his son.

John Locke

The foundation of every state is the education of its youth.

Diogenes

The direction in which education starts a man will determine his future life.

Plato

Pay attention to the young, and make them just as good as possible.

Socrates

Miscellaneous

They that wait upon the Lord shall renew their strength; they shall mount up with wings as eagles; they shall run, and not be weary, and they shall walk, and not faint.

Bible, Isaiah 40:31

The heights by great men reached and kept
Were not attained by sudden flight,
But they, while their companions slept,
Were toiling upward in the night.

Henry Wadsworth Longfellow

He clasps the crag with crooked hands:
Close to the sun in lonely lands,
Ring'd with the azure world, he stands.
The wrinkled sea beneath him crawls;
He watches from his mountain walls,
And like a thunderbolt he falls.

Alfred, Lord Tennyson

With storm-daring pinion and sun-gazing eye,
The gray forest eagle is king of the sky!

Alfred B. Street

It is not the critic who counts, not the man who points out how the strong man stumbled, or where the doer of deeds could have done better. The credit belongs to the man who is actually in the arena: whose face is marred by dust and sweat and blood: who strives valiantly: who errs and comes short again and again: who knows the great enthusiasms, the great devotions, and spends himself in worthy cause: who, at the best, knows in the end the triumph of high achievements: and who, at the worst, if he fails, at least fails while daring greatly, so that his place shall never be with those cold and timid souls who know neither victory nor defeat.

Theodore Roosevelt

D. Props

Although not required for all courts of honor, props can greatly increase the effectiveness of any ceremony. A variety of props are discussed below. Some are designed to be integral parts of certain ceremonies; others merely serve as decorations.

Before you spend a lot of time and money building props, check with your local council and with other troops in your area. You may be able to borrow everything you need.

Candelabrums

A candelabrum is essential to many of the Scouting segments in Chapter 4. Your candelabrum should hold 12 candles representing the points of the Scout Law and three candles representing the parts of the Scout Oath (duty to God and country, duty to others, and duty to self). Two versions are illustrated here.

Lighted Sign

The sign below is designed to be illuminated section by section as you discuss the ranks leading up to Eagle. (You could also make a lighted sign showing the parts of the Eagle badge.)

The front of the sign is made of translucent plastic or fiberglass with the badges painted on. The box is sectioned off so that each section can be illuminated independently.

To get the images onto the plastic, project them using an opaque projector. Then trace and paint the images.

Each light should have a separate switch. I recommend putting an in-line switch near the end of each cord and plugging all the cords into a power strip or multi-plug adapter. Make the cords long enough that someone can stand off-stage and control the lights.

Eagle "Jigsaw" Sign

One council I know of has a large white metal sign, about five feet tall, with an Eagle badge on it. Each part of the badge is actually a separate piece of wood with magnets on the back. Since the pieces are easy to take off and put on, this sign could be used instead of the lighted sign described above. In your ceremony, as you discuss each part of the Eagle badge, you could stick that part of the badge on the sign.

To create a sign like this, use an opaque projector to magnify a picture of the badge onto thick plywood. Cut the pieces using a scroll saw. Make five separate pieces: the scroll and knot, the eagle pendant, and each section of the ribbon. A shop that makes magnetic signs for cars and trucks can supply magnetic sheeting for the backs of the pieces.

Presentation Pillow

During the presentation phase of the ceremony, some troops bring the awards forward on a fancy pillow instead of just having them lying on a table. If you have someone in your troop who does needlepoint or cross-stitch, ask them to make an Eagle pillow for you. (The BSA once published a helpful booklet called BSA Emblems in Counted Cross Stitch, but it's now out of print.)

Inexpensive Backdrop

If the room where you're holding your court of honor has a stage, you can create an inexpensive but effective backdrop using a slide or video projector and a white sheet. Hang the sheet vertically about halfway to the back of the stage. Set up your projector behind the sheet, pointing toward it. By projecting a slide of an Eagle badge (reversed) onto the sheet, you'll create a good backdrop and not have to worry about people walking between the projector and the screen.

You can get a slide made for a few dollars at a good photo shop, but these days, most people use video projectors instead.

The same thing could also be done using an overhead projector. The slide-projector version is illustrated on the next page.

E. The History of the Eagle Scout Award

In the Beginning

Considering the central importance of the Eagle Scout Award in Scouting, it's interesting to note that the badge was not part of the program as it was first envisioned. Robert Baden-Powell's *Scouting for Boys* included only three ranks: Tenderfoot, Second Class, and First Class.

This scheme was repeated in the proof edition of the first American *Handbook for Boys*, compiled by Ernest Thompson Seton in 1910. Seton did add the Silver Wolf award, to be given to any Scout who earned all 14 "badges of merit" – Ambulance, Fireman, Cyclist, Clerk, Signaller, Pioneer, Seaman, Marksman, Master-at-Arms, Stalker, Gardener, Horseman, Electrician, and Musician. However, neither the Silver Wolf nor the badges of merit were ever produced.

By the time the *Handbook for Boys* was ready for the public, several changes had been made. There were now 57 merit badges, the Life and Star ranks (in that order) had been added after First Class, and the Silver Wolf had been replaced by the Eagle. (The June 1911 *Handbook for Boys*, however, still included the Silver Wolf.)

According to the August 1911 *Handbook*, "Any first-class scout qualifying for twenty-one merit badges will be entitled to wear the highest scout merit badge. This is an eagle's head in silver, and represents the all-round perfect scout." On the same page was a drawing of the badge, an eagle in flight – not the eagle's head that the text described – suspended from a single-color ribbon.

The First Eagle Scout

Neither version of the Eagle badge from the *Handbook for Boys* was actually produced. In fact, no Eagle badges were made until 1912, when Arthur R. Eldred of Troop 1 in Oceanside, New York, became the first Eagle Scout.

Eldred was personally examined by Chief Scout Executive James E. West, Chief Scout Ernest Thompson Seton, National Scout Commissioner Daniel Carter Beard, and Wilbert E. Longfellow of the U.S. Volunteer Life Saving Corps, who had written parts of the *Handbook for Boys*. Eldred became the first Eagle Scout on August 21, 1912, and received his award on September 2.

The badge Eldred received that Labor Day (now on display at the National Scouting Museum in Irving, Texas) was produced by the T.H. Foley Company of New York, New York. Although rather crudely made, the badge closely resembled the badges still produced today.

Requirement Changes

At first, Scouts did not have to complete any specific merit badges to earn Eagle itself, although to become Life Scouts they had to earn First Aid, Athletics, Life-saving, Personal Health, and Public Health.

By 1915, however, 11 specific merit badges were required for Eagle, along with 10 elective badges. The required merit badges were First Aid, Life Saving, Personal Health, Public Health, Cooking, Camping, Civics, Bird Study, Pathfinding, Pioneering, and Athletics or Physical Development. Since then, there has always been a list of Eagle-required merit badges. (The list has changed several times as various aspects of Scouting have been emphasized or de-emphasized.)

In 1924, the Life and Star ranks were reversed. In 1926, the requirements for the top three ranks were expanded to include more than just earning merit badges. Now to become an Eagle Scout, a boy had to serve as a First Class Scout for a year, "showing that he has actually put into practice the ideals and principles of the Scout Oath and Law, the motto 'Be Prepared' and the Daily Good Turn and has made an earnest effort to develop his leadership ability."

Another change in 1926 was the addition of Eagle palms, awards beyond Eagle given for earning additional merit badges and continuing to put into practice the ideals of Scouting.

For the first four decades of Scouting, adult leaders could participate in the advancement program. That practice ended in 1952, after which time all requirements had to be completed by a Scout's eighteenth birthday.

The Modern Eagle Award

In 1965, three requirements were added that greatly expanded what it meant to be an Eagle Scout. With the addition of these requirements, the modern Eagle award was born.

Before 1965, an Eagle candidate was expected to "work actively as a leader in meetings, outdoor activities, and service projects" in his troop. Starting that year, however, he had to serve at least six months in a position such as patrol leader, quartermaster, or junior assistant Scoutmaster.

Another new requirement was the Eagle service project: "While a Life Scout, plan, develop, and carry out a service project helpful to your church or synagogue, school, or community approved in advance by your Scoutmaster."

Finally, a conference with the Scoutmaster was required. At this conference the Scout was to discuss his future in Scouting, what the Eagle badge meant to him, and what the ideals of Scouting meant to him and how he tried to live up to them.

Few other significant changes have been made since 1965. A total of 24 merit badges was required from 1972 to 1979, and the list of required merit badges has fluctuated (most recently in 1999), but the core requirements have remained constant.

Medals, Patches, Ribbon Bars, and Knots

Just as the requirements for the Eagle Scout Award have changed over the years, so has the badge itself. Terry Grove, in his book *A Comprehensive Guide to the Eagle Scout Award*, has identified 16 major types of Eagle medals. Variations include the design of the eagle pendant, whether the back of the eagle is detailed, whether "BSA" appears across the eagle's front, the design of the scroll, and the types of metal used.

The pocket patch, first introduced in 1924, has appeared in eight different versions. Interestingly, the current patch is actually the same design that was used from 1956 to 1972.

From 1934 to 1946, Scouts and Scouters could wear a ribbon bar, similar to those found on military uniforms, to show that they had earned the Eagle award. In 1946, all ribbon bars were discontinued; the red, white, and blue Eagle square-knot patch was introduced in 1947.

Beyond the Eagle

We often say in Eagle courts of honor that there is no end to the Eagle Scout trail. In 1925, two organizations were formed to keep Eagles (and other former Scouts) active in Scouting and in their communities.

Alpha Phi Omega, a college fraternity for former Scouts, was founded at Lafayette College in Easton, Pennsylvania. Scouting experience is no longer a requirement for membership, but APO's focus is still service, and the fraternity still has good relations with the Boy Scouts of America.

The other group formed in 1925 was the Knights of Dunamis. This organization for Eagle Scouts was founded by San Francisco Scout Executive Raymond O. Hansen. In 1972, the Knights of Dunamis and several local council Eagle associations merged to form the National Eagle Scout Association.

NESA's goal is to keep Eagle Scouts informed about and involved in Scouting. The organization publishes the quarterly *Eagle Scout Magazine* and regularly informs local councils of newly-identified Eagles in their areas. Recently, NESA has expanded its website to include social-networking features.

Eagle Scouts Today

A few years ago, NESA reported that the average Scout takes 4 years, 11 months, and 16 days to become an Eagle Scout. NESA also reported that 78 percent of Eagle Scouts were Webelos Scouts, and 71 percent had earned the Arrow of Light, Cub Scouting's highest award.

A milestone was reached in 1982, when Alexander Holsinger, of Normal, Illinois, became the one-millionth Eagle Scout. Nearly three decades later, in 2009, Anthony Thomas of Lakeville, Minnesota, became the two-millionth recipient of the Eagle Scout Award. Today, more than 50,000 Scouts become Eagles annually; many of them are the sons and grandsons of Eagle Scouts.

Since Arthur Eldred received the first Eagle Scout Award in 1912, the Scouting program and the Eagle badge itself have undergone many changes. But one thing has remained constant: the Eagle Scout still represents the best that Scouting has to offer.

About the Author

In a Scouting career spanning more than a quarter of a century, Mark Ray has participated in the program at almost every level: as a Scout, Scout parent, district executive, Wood Badge and national jamboree staff member, Philmont Training Center faculty member, and Cub Scout, Boy Scout, and Venturing volunteer. Mark is an Eagle Scout, a Vigil Honor member of the Order of the Arrow, and a recipient of the Silver Beaver Award. A freelance writer based in Louisville, Kentucky, Mark is also the author of *The Scoutmaster's Other Handbook*.

You can write to Mark at:

Resources for Boy Scouting
P.O. Box 22314
Louisville, KY 40252
info@eaglebook.com

Find More Resources Online
at www.eaglebook.com

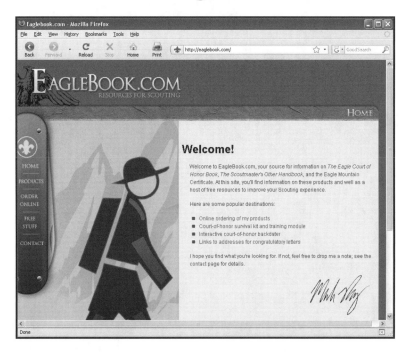

Visit **www.eaglebook.com** for even more information on planning great Eagle courts of honor. At the site, you can access free court of honor tips, download a court of honor training module, order additional copies of *The Eagle Court of Honor Book*, and learn about the unique, personalized Eagle Mountain Presentation Certificate.

The scripts and ceremony segments found in this book are available online at **www.eaglebook.com/scripts/**.

The site also features information on *The Scoutmaster's Other Handbook*, including links to dozens of websites discussed in that book, and on other books and videos of interest to Scouters.

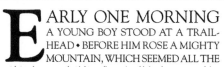

EARLY ONE MORNING
A YOUNG BOY STOOD AT A TRAIL-
HEAD • BEFORE HIM ROSE A MIGHTY
MOUNTAIN, WHICH SEEMED ALL THE
mightier when compared with his smallness • A trail led to the mountain and then
up it to incredible heights before vanishing in the clouds • On this trail the boy could
see other boys and young men, some of whom turned and beckoned him to follow •
The boy began to climb, refusing perhaps to believe that he could ever reach the top
• At first the trail rose gently and the boy had many companions • But soon he began
to sweat and breathe heavily and many of his companions turned away • And still the
boy climbed • At times he climbed quickly • At times he climbed slowly • At times he
had to go down a little way to find another path or stop a while to catch his breath •
But still he climbed • The trail became steeper, the air thinner, but the climber scarcely
noticed for he had, along the way, become stronger of body and hardier of spirit •
And still he climbed • And finally in the cool peace of eveningtime, he stood alone at
the top of the world and looked around him • To the left he saw a fiery golden sunset
• To the right he saw a diamond-studded, silky-black night sky • Behind him he saw
the trail that he had followed and the hikers who were following in his footsteps •
And in front of him he saw another mountain • And another • And another • And a
whole procession of mountains marching off to the horizon • But the young man (for
now he *was* a man) knew that none of these other mountains was insurmountable,
that all could and would be climbed • For he had learned many skills in the climbing
of the first mountain, and he would carry those skills with him long after this mountain was forgotten • And besides, he could
begin climbing the next mountain
tomorrow • Tonight he would rest and
celebrate and ponder the journey that
he had completed • And so, too,
should *we* rest and celebrate and
honor this fine young man
Jonathan Springer
as he stands at the top of the world
and looks around him ⌐♯⌐

February 8, 2012

The Eagle Mountain Certificate

Now you can honor your favorite Scout with a unique, personalized copy of the "Legend of Eagle Mountain," as featured in *The
Eagle Court of Honor Book.* This certificate tells the story of a boy's
climb to Scouting's highest peak: the Eagle Scout rank. Each
certificate is personalized with the recipient's name and the court-
of-honor or board-of-review date.

The Eagle Mountain Presentation Certificate is printed on hand-
some parchment-style paper and is available in two sizes: 8" x 10"
and 8.5" x 11". It's the perfect gift for any new (or not-so-new)
recipient of the Eagle badge.

For more information on the Eagle Mountain Certificate, or to
place an order, visit **www.eaglebook.com**.

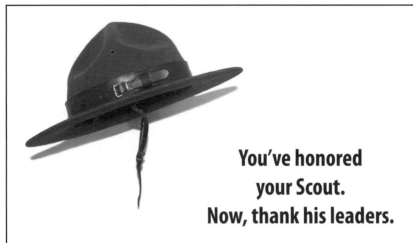

Order Form

Please print.

Name _____

Address _____

_____

E-mail _____

Phone (_____) _____ Date _____

Qty.		Price Each	Total
	The Eagle Court of Honor Book	$14.95	
	The Scoutmaster's Other Handbook	$14.95	
	Shipping Method (check one)	❏ Priority ❏ Media	
	Shipping & Handling (see chart)		
	6% Sales Tax (Kentucky residents only)		
	Grand Total		

Shipping & Handling		
Shipping Method	**First Book**	**Each Add'l Book**
Priority Mail (2-3 days)	$6.25	$1.50
Media Mail (6-7 days)	$3.50	$1.00

Mail completed order form with check or money order (payable to Mark Ray) to:

**Mark Ray
P. O. Box 22314
Louisville, KY 40252-0314**

Note: Prices are subject to change without notice. For more information (including discounts for bookstores and Scout Shops), call 502-327-9229 or e-mail to **info@eaglebook.com**. Online ordering is available at **www.eaglebook.com**.